how to
find God
in everything

Amoda Maa Jeevan is a spiritual teacher and author with 10 years' experience of leading personal transformation groups. She currently lives in London, with her partner Kavi, with whom she teaches some of her work.

how to
find God
in everything

*An Invitation to Awaken to Your True Nature
and Transform Your World*

AMODA MAA JEEVAN

Distributed in the USA and Canada by Sterling Publishing Co., Inc.
387 Park Avenue South, New York, NY 10016

This edition first published in the UK and USA 2008 by
Watkins Publishing, Sixth Floor, Castle House,
75–76 Wells Street, London W1T 3QH

10 9 8 7 6 5 4 3 2 1

Designed and typeset by Jen Cogliantry

Printed in China by Imago

Library of Congress Cataloging-in-Publication Data Available

ISBN10: 1-905857-50-0
ISBN13: 978-1-905857-50-0

www.watkinspublishing.co.uk

For information about custom editions, special sales, premium and
corporate purchases, please contact Sterling Special Sales
Department at 800-805-5489 or specialsales@sterlingpub.com.

Contents

Acknowledgments

This book has taken a long time to gestate – and an even longer time to write. Along the way, there have been a number of people who have supported me, inspired me and been instrumental in my evolution both as a writer and as an authentic human being.

Those who have assisted directly include, first and foremost, writers' coach Julia McCutchen whose initial enthusiasm fanned the flames of possibility and whose sensitive feedback and gentle advice have been invaluable. A thousand thank yous, Julia – I doubt this book would have seen the light of day without you. In addition, I am indebted to my editor, Michael Mann, for his vision and conviction for this project. I also thank the team at Watkins and Duncan Baird for your input.

Those who have been a part of the process indirectly include – on the earthly plane – Richard Rudd whose genecode revelations came like a thunderbolt from the heavens and awakened me to my true purpose, and Drs Pankaj and Smita Naram and their team at Ayushakti Ayurvedic Clinic in Mumbai whose expertise and loving care rejuvenated my body, mind and soul and helped me see the world with fresh eyes. On the spiritual plane, I am eternally grateful to Ramana Maharshi whose vibration of Truth penetrated deep into my being, stripped me of what was false and catapulted me into a new phase of life, and to Osho whose ever-present Love continues to burn bright in my heart.

I'd also like to thank all those who've attended my classes, workshops and retreats during the years of Moving Creations. I am truly blessed by both the sublime and the crazy times we have shared! And I thank each and every one of you for your patience whilst I – and my work – have gone through countless transformations. I especially thank Zen whose unwavering devotion constantly delights me.

Last, but certainly not least, there are not enough words to thank the two most important people in my life, both of whom have contributed to my growth in very different ways. These are my mother, who unceasingly loves me and Kavi Jezzie Hockaday, my beloved, my creative partner and my true friend.

A Changing World

It is time to tell it like it is. Each of us is being called to awaken to our true nature, to dive deep inside and find God in the one place we have forgotten to look: in our hearts. As life hurtles into the 21st century we are each called to make a difference to our world by choosing love over fear.

Every day we are bombarded by news of violence, corruption, war, and terrorism. By now we all know that the political, economic and environmental climates are becoming increasingly unstable. And we can't deny that for the first time in recorded history the threat of total planetary annihilation looms on the horizon.

We must face the unavoidable truth: the world is in crisis and nothing short of a total spiritual transformation will avert the catastrophe that lies ahead. We are being called to create a new world paradigm: one based on love instead of fear. Fear closes our hearts and shuts God out. We forget our alignment to a harmonious vertical reality in which we are one with All That Is and fall into a fragmented horizontal reality in which we are separate from each other, from the world, from Life, and from Source. Surely, the mess we have got ourselves into is a by-product of the fear-based paradigm we have been living in for so long?

We need to wake up from the slumber of forgetfulness and remember who we really are.

I believe – as do many others – that only a radical shift of perception from a *self*-centered to a *God*-centered world-view will transform our reality from one of separation to one of unity. I believe that if we can see through the eyes of the heart we will reclaim our divine inheritance and create Heaven on Earth.

We need to wake up from the slumber of forgetfulness and remember who we really are.

Waking Up in the 21st Century

The belief that we are small and powerless in the face of Life is a lie that has kept us asleep for thousands of years. But God is knocking on the door now, urging us to wake up to the full glory of our true nature.

We can no longer wait for the politicians to stop bickering, for the environmentalists to think of a solution or for world leaders to save us. We need to stop believing that someone else has the answer and actually become the change we want to see. The future is in our hands.

Amidst all the chaos we are being given the opportunity for liberation. When we stop looking outside ourselves for something to make us feel better, safer, stronger, richer or happier, and instead open to the deepest knowing in our beings, we realize our essential nature and change our reality. Each of us is the perfection of this very moment. The kingdom of Heaven lies within: what we seek is what we are. And what we are lies in our hearts.

The stark naked truth is that each and every one of us is a manifestation of God. This very realization has the power to change the world. When you see God in everyone, all separation dissolves. When you see beyond gender, race, class, wealth, job-title or any other label, all boundaries

The kingdom of Heaven lies within: what we seek is what we are. And what we are lies in our hearts.

evaporate and you find yourself floating in the nameless silence of Being that is your essential nature.

We stand on the brink of a revolution in consciousness that has the power to transform our world. It is up to each of us to choose whether we are a part of this change.

The Collective Vision

Several years ago I had a visionary experience that is still as vivid today as it was then.

In this vision, I am walking through the Valley of Death, a landscape so barren it is devoid of all hope. Surrounded by hungry ghosts and tortured souls, a cold darkness creeps into my veins and my body feels heavy with the suffering of all humankind. All I want to do is lie down and die. As the flame of life flickers one last time in the center of my heart, I look skywards as if to say: "Thank you for my life so far, now it is time to go." But just as I am about to shut my eyes forever more, I see a faint glow in the distance ... like a dream of a brighter future. But this is no dream; my eyes are wide open. Rooted to the spot, I watch in disbelief as the light spreads before me like a carpet. I summon all my strength and prepare to wearily climb the golden steps that appear in front of me. I am amazed how light I feel. "I have died and gone to Heaven!" I shout. But the steps are real and I have to keep climbing without looking back. With each footstep I become increasingly humbled by this state of grace, for I have become a Child of God.

When I arrive at the top and stand at my Father's feet, I am innocent and naked as a baby. There is nothing to hide. I climb into His lap in such a state of humility and surrender that I am ready to die once more for this love, to sleep sweetly in His arms forever. But no sooner do I lay down my head than I merge with Him completely. And in doing so, I achieve the Sacred Union in which *I am* Him. And in that same instant, I am also His Consort, the Holy Mother who sits by His side. From my womb springs a Golden Child and from my breasts flows the Milk of Human Kindness that creates an eternal river to ease humanity's suffering. And, in time, the Valley of Death becomes the Land of Milk and Honey ... a true Paradise here on Earth.

This vision forms the crux of this book. What it says is that the journey of transformation means becoming naked.

If we want to move towards the light, we need to stop hiding behind the mask of ego and become as little children, ready to bare ourselves completely. Walking on our path through life with the innocence of an open heart is the only way to transform our suffering. And this means steadfastly taking one step at a time. It's something we need to do as a day-to-day, moment-to-moment practice. It's not easy because fear pulls us back. It requires us to stay resolutely present without looking backwards or forwards. What this means is that we neither give in to being a victim of the past nor do we grasp for some imaginary goal in the future. Ultimately, it means sacrificing our ego on the altar of God.

God is that which is bigger than us, the Great Mystery, the One That Is All. The reward when we totally surrender to God is the unlocking of the spiritual power of our dormant masculine and feminine energies. This is the alchemical marriage of the Father and the Mother from whom we are reborn as the Golden Child. In other words, when we fully embody the depth of our masculine energy and the openness of our feminine energy, the seed of awakening grows within us and we give birth to our essential self. This is the divine spark of infinite creative potential that illuminates us from within. It is something that, again, we need to develop as an on-going practice.

Every moment is an opportunity to awaken to our true identity. And in this remembrance we are made complete. The trinity of Father, Mother and Golden Child is both a symbol of our innate wholeness and of our essential holiness. It is the sacred space of oneness within our hearts from which compassion flows for all that exists.

This story not only urges us to wake up and become who we really are in order to transform our lives, but it is also a vision of the future. The Valley of Death is both the personal hell-realm of the ego and also the samsara of a world hell-bent on destruction. The alchemical marriage of the Father and the Mother is both the integration of our inner male and female and also the healing of the masculine-feminine split we see in man versus woman, intellect versus intuition, science versus mysticism, and religion versus nature. The Land of Milk and Honey is both the full flowering of our individual creative potential, and also the creation of a new world built on foundations of Love and Truth.

What's surprised me about this vision – perhaps more than anything else – is the emphasis on God. Like so many

*God is that which is bigger than us,
the Great Mystery, the One That Is All.*

of us raised against a backdrop of religious dogma, I banned the word God from my vocabulary a long time ago. It was not until quite recently that I saw God not as some abstract concept but as a direct experience. God is synonymous with Life and the more I open to receive every aspect of Existence in its fullness, the more *this* moment explodes with vibrant intimacy. My relationship with God is an adventure into love that brings me closer to myself and closer to everyone and everything in my life. That which I have been seeking is what I am, for God is my essential nature.

And yours too.

A Tidal Wave of Love

How we see God is crucial to what kind of world we live in. The global transformation we need so much will only happen when we stop searching for God outside of ourselves. God does not live up there in the clouds, waiting till you arrive at Heaven's door before He reveals himself; He is to be found resting inside every experience you have. God resides in the heart of every action, every thought, every feelings and every breath.

Recognizing the divine spark that animates each moment brings God down to Earth and heals the separation between matter and spirit that is the root cause of our suffering.

Imagine how different both our inner world and the outer world would be if we could see God in everyone and everything! I expect it would be a world in which fear, struggle and guilt disappeared and in which war, violence and greed were a thing of the past. I expect it would be a world in which we are free to express our unlimited nature and empowered to manifest our highest potential. And I expect it would be a world resonating with the majesty of its own beauty and celebrating its own joyful existence.

This book shows you that every experience in your life is a calling from God, an invitation to dive deeper into the mystery of Life as *it is now*. Choosing love over fear in every moment and in every circumstance – however difficult or painful – transforms the misery of closedness into the miracle of openness. Every interaction we have with every aspect of our life provides a doorway to the Divine ... if only we would recognize it.

Part I of this book explores how Life itself is a calling from God and how the journey of transformation requires the openness of your being – or Love – and the depth of your presence or Truth. Each and every one of us is a part of the collective vision and we are each being called to awaken to Love and Truth in every moment of our lives in order to transform our personal and global reality.

In Part II, I introduce the Seven Gateways to God. Each one of these explores an aspect of human life ranging from the tangibility of our physical nature to the intangibility of spirit. And in each gateway, I show you how to unlock the secret of God using the golden keys of Love and Truth. At the end of each chapter is an invitation to try a simple exercise that offers you a glimpse of the secret inside each gateway. You can choose to try it once or you can practice it regularly to deepen your experience. You can also use the companion CD 'Seven Gateways to God' which guides you through each meditation. (Details are at the end of the book.)

Every aspect of Life – from the mundane to the

transcendent – offers an opportunity for transformation. The traditional spiritual path that considers everyday matters such as health, finances, work, family and relationship to be distractions is no longer relevant. What we need today is a truly holistic spirituality. What we need is not only a rainbow-colored Universal Love that prays for peace but also a love that is practical. We need a love that cherishes the physical vehicle of our soul because a healthy body is more able to carry out God's work. We need a love that is unafraid of handling money because global wealth so badly needs redistribution. We need a love that always thinks ahead and starts creating now what future generations will need. In other words, we need Love in Action.

And neither is it enough to sit silently in the emptiness of Ultimate Truth: we also need a truth that serves our everyday reality. We need a truth that speaks of our innermost feelings, that expresses the full range of emotions, and that has the

God resides in the heart of every action, every thought, every feeling and every breath.

courage to drop pretences in order to reveal the tenderness of an open heart. What we really need is a truth that bridges the gap between the imperfection of our humanness and the perfection of our God-essence.

I believe there is a wave of global transformation – a tsunami of love – coming our way. It requires trust that we will be carried to the other shore safe, whole, and complete. The challenge we face is to dive into love even when fear screams at us to run and hide, to open our hearts even in the midst of hell. We are each being called to give up small *me* and become one with the vastness of Being that is who you really are! Life itself is calling you. God is calling you. *You* are calling yourself to remember!

The vision of a brighter future belongs to every one of us. Will you choose love over fear? Will you choose to be who you really are?

My hope is that this book speaks to you ... that you hear the call. And have the courage to make the leap from your head to your heart.

PART I:

How to Find God

Chapter 1

THE CALL TO
EMBRACE LIFE

Every experience of your life is a calling from God. Every experience – whether it be pleasurable or painful – is an invitation to embrace the fullness and depth of this moment as it is now. Deep intimacy with this moment offers the promise of liberation. It is an invitation to your true nature.

Beyond appearances, beyond what comes and goes, is the *you* that does not change: the *you* that is neither *this* nor *that*, but simply *is*. You cannot find this part of you by looking into the future or by dwelling in the past because time is an illusion that takes you away from the reality of *now*. The truth of who you are can only be found in the absolute presence of *this* moment. In this moment you are whole: there is nothing that can be added or taken away. And, in this moment, you are holy: you are not separate from the sacredness of spirit. You are, in fact, a divine creation of unlimited potential. In this perfect moment you are at one with yourself, at one with Life and at one with God. For God is your essential nature. And mine. And everyone else's too.

God is the Infinite Intelligence that is the Source of Creation, the One that is the Totality of Existence. Everything that exists is a manifestation of the One. And this includes every human being, every living creature, everything that we create, every event, action, thought and feeling. God is Life itself. And Life is simply that which *is*.

The closer we get to experiencing the pure, unadulterated is-ness of Life, the closer we get to God.

Every experience of your life is a calling from God.

The Illusion of A Perfect Life

Most of us spend a vast proportion of our time trying to control life. We want it to be pleasant and fun. We want to have all the good things. But however rich, successful or powerful we are, we have to admit somewhere deep down inside that life is not always so easy. Disappointment, failure, loss, and hurt are all a part of the human experience. Pain is woven into the fabric of life. However much we want to make things nice, we simply cannot control how things turn out.

The fact is life is full of contradictions. It can be fascinating in its intricate complexity and wonderful in its ability to uplift our souls. But it can also be agonizing in its harsh unpredictability and terrible in its capacity to take us to the rough edge that fills us with dread. I'm sure we've all experienced times when life takes an unexpected turn and we find ourselves facing the unknown. This is when we want to turn back the clock, when we want to run away and hide. Or perhaps we just want to curl up and die. We will do anything but stay where we are and *feel* the discomfort.

Today's fast-track world does little to encourage us to trust the ebb and flow of life. Modern media sells us the dream of a perfect life in which we have everything we want and only good things happen. We know that life isn't really like this but still we cling to the dream.

I spent most of my 20s trying to have a perfect life. I thought that if I had the best clothes, the latest hairstyle and the top qualifications, I'd be happy. I was so busy chasing a glittering dream that I missed the raw beauty of life right under my nose. On the surface I appeared well-groomed and successful but inside I was a mess.

It took an almighty psychological breakdown to smash the illusion and bring me to my senses. Within a few months my perfect outer world crumbled and I was left with literally nothing. And yet, even though this was one of the most materially barren periods of my life it was also one of the most fertile in terms of emotional and spiritual growth. When I finally saw that the treasure I was seeking could only be found by plumbing the depths of my inner world, a new chapter of my life began.

Most of us, at some time or another, seek solace in shopping and socializing, cling to security through insurance schemes and pension plans and maybe cushion discomfort with intoxicants and painkillers. When we are young it's

Life and death, gain and loss, joy and sorrow ... all these are a part of the cycle of Existence.

easy to fool ourselves that life can be pain-free. But all the glamour and wealth in the world cannot hide the fact that one day each and every one of us will get old and experience some degree of difficulty. Eventually, we *all* have to face the inevitability of our own death.

Life and death, gain and loss, joy and sorrow ... all these are a part of the cycle of Existence. Behind the modern-day façade of Happily Ever After, the wheel of Life continues to turn. As surely as the sun rises, the sun sets, and as surely as the tide flows in, the tide flows out. Change is an inevitable part of life. Trying to control the natural flow just because you want things to be other than the way they are doesn't work in the long run. Wanting things to be bigger, better, easier, and safer does not make you happy.

And neither does it make you free.

Resistance to Now

It is precisely our wanting things to be different that creates our suffering. It is not the hardship, discomfort or pain itself that is the cause of suffering – although it appears to be – but the *resistance* to fully experiencing it.

Every time we close down to numb the pain or tighten to defend against discomfort, we resist what is actually happening *now*. And in turning away from *this* moment, we give our power away to something outside of ourselves: we become victims of our circumstances. Not only do we get caught in a merry-go-round of cravings and aversions but we also end up fighting the current of life. Instead of going with the flow, we end up swimming upstream. Eventually this is exhausting!

Seeking safety and pleasure as a short-cut to happiness is an illusion that limits the breadth and depth of our experience and impoverishes our spirit. Even the tiniest step away from Life *as it is* now clips our wings and dulls our shine. Whenever we move away from the edge, whenever we shrink, collapse or space out – whenever we do anything rather than stay *exactly* where we are and *feel* it – we move away from our true nature.

Every time you create a storyline – about yourself, about someone else, about the world, about Life or about God – you can be sure you have forgotten your true nature. One of the most common storylines is the Poor Me syndrome. If in the face of life's challenges your favorite response is: "Why me?" or "What's wrong with me? I must be stupid/bad/ unlovable," or "What have I done wrong? I'm being punished by my friends/family/boss/life/God" – or any variation on this theme – then you can be sure you identify with Poor Me. The other most common response is the Blame syndrome: if you frequently say or think: "It's your fault, you must be wrong!" or "Life's difficult, it stinks!" or "The devil made me do it," or "God shouldn't have let this happen" – or any variation on this theme – then you are caught in the Blame syndrome.

Dig deep beneath the surface and you will find that we all succumb to such storylines, at least in some areas of our lives. I know the Poor Me syndrome well as I spent many years believing everything was my fault. As soon as I was faced with a challenge I'd retract from feeling the full depth of it. Rather than feel angry, sad, hurt or any other uncomfortable emotion, I'd collapse into "I'm a bad person" and stay depressed for days.

What I have learnt is that in retracting from Life *as it is now*, we shrink to fit the shell of our ego. Ego always seeks to protect itself from an imaginary threat. It lives in the personal realm of *me* and *mine* and so creates a separation between *me* and *you*, *me* and *the world*, *me* and *Life*. In other words, ego lives in the illusory world of duality. You know you are operating from the personal when things appear black and white. Or when you judge someone as *right* or *wrong*. Or when you label something as *good* or *bad*. The ego will do anything rather than just be OK with things as they are.

When you resist *what is*, you forget who you are and become less than whole. And you also become less than holy. This deep alienation from our essential self and the essence of Life is the cause of all personal suffering – including illness – as well as the violence, rape, war, greed, consumerism and nihilism we see running rampant across the world. Ultimately, it is the separation from God that is the root cause of all suffering. When we lose our connection with Source that creates us, we forget that we are all one and become divided from all Life, from each other and from ourselves. When we fail to see God in everyone and everything, we close our hearts and live in fear. And in a fear-based world, our vision is clouded. It's as if we are caught in a spell that keeps us in limitation.

Breaking this spell of separation requires a conscious choice to overcome our resistance to *now*.

Breaking the Spell of Separation

We have been conditioned to protect, defend and armor ourselves so that we stay safe. We have learnt to put up walls around our hearts when someone gets too close and pull blinkers over our eyes so that we don't see what we don't like. These patterns are so ingrained that they happen unconsciously.

If we want to empower ourselves to be all that we truly are, we need to make some degree of effort to overcome this inertia. It's easy to think that giving in to old patterns requires less energy, but the small amount of effort it takes to overcome this sleepiness actually allows us access to boundless energy that is at our source. I distinctly remember the day one of my teachers told me that if I could just put all my attention into the very moment that was presenting itself to me, then I would stop feeling like I was carrying a bag of woes uphill and instead feel like I was gliding freely in the flow.

Making the choice to wake up means breaking out of your self-imposed prison. When you stop clinging to the safety of your habitual self-protectiveness and let go into the river of Life, you experience the perfection of *this* moment *as it is* ... in all its glory and all its horror.

In awakening, you return to your natural state of divinity. You drop the layers of conditioning that mask the luminescent beauty of your essence and become who you really are. You are, in fact, greater than you think you are. The truth is, *you are God!* Knowing you are God may sound like an extraordinary revelation. And it *is* in the sense that so few of us realize it. But it is also very ordinary: it is a return to our natural state. It is not that we suddenly sprout wings and have magical powers! We do not become something other than what we already are. We just let go of what we are not.

Realizing you are God is simply a shift from the personal perspective of *me* and *mine* to the universal perspective of *we are all manifestations* of God. Ultimately, it's a shift from the bondage of conditioned thinking to the liberation of being. We don't have to wait till we are *good enough* or *spiritual enough* to realize we are God. In fact, the shift from thinking to being can only happen right here and *now*. The freedom that you seek lies within, in the very heart of each moment. God is inside each thought, each feeling, each word, and each deed.

In *this* perfect moment, you, me and everyone else are both whole and holy.

The Miracle of Openness

When you're teetering on the edge and there's no escape, do you harden into "I'm not going to move a muscle," or do you soften into "Let's see where this takes me?" When your back is really up against it and every fiber of your being is screaming, do you close into "I won't let this touch me," or do you open into "Maybe I'll let this in and make friends with it?" In every circumstance, you can jump into defensive reaction using those same old strategies. Or you can pause, take a deep breath and allow the miracle of something new to take place. Which do you choose?

Well, let me tell you something: the first option prolongs the agony. When you shut down or tighten to protect yourself, pain becomes a curse that follows you around. It's surprising how many of us don't actually know this. Whatever you resist will always come back to you ... over and over again. Any retraction from pain creates a knot of tension that cries out for attention. You can choose to turn away from it and let your life contort itself around the jagged edges of your resistance, but you only end up trapped by your refusal to soften into openness. Over time, your mind becomes twisted into storylines, your body gnarled with locked emotion and your spirit yearning for the fullness of love.

Luckily, the second option – softening into the pain – creates a miracle. When you allow yourself to relax into what hurts, a doorway opens to a new level of experience that enriches your life and transforms pain into a blessing. Whatever shape your pain may take, you can choose to relax, breathe into it and flow with its contours. What matters is not whether you can make it go away, fix it or resolve it, but the breadth of your *openness* around the pain and the depth of your *presence* amidst the pain. Whether it is the sharp remnant of a relationship that's ended, the dark shadow of a childhood trauma, or the consistent gnaw of a debilitating illness, you can choose to accept the pattern of your life in *this* moment.

Don't get acceptance mixed up with resignation! The tired sigh of "Oh well, that's how things are" may seem like a sign that you have made peace with things. But if you're really honest, you'll admit that deep inside you are still resisting *what is*. Acceptance, on the other hand, means a conscious "Yes!" to Life *as it is now*. It's a clear-cut choice between love and fear: fear creates contraction and separation, love creates openness and oneness.

It's a strange thing, but the wider you open to let Life in, the more meaningful and sacred, as well as the more playful and delightful, it becomes. In acceptance, Life becomes a multi-dimensional game to be enjoyed, a divine play or *leela*. This is a wonderful paradox that is one of the secrets of the spiritual path!

Conscious surrender to *what is* is the only way to surf the razor's edge to freedom.

Embracing Pain as a Friend

The good news is it actually gets easier to embrace pain the more you do it. It's like a muscle that gets stronger the more you use it. Eventually pain is no longer the enemy but a friend along the journey of life. I wish someone had told me this before, but like everyone else, I had to learn the hard way.

The biggest lesson came when my ten-year marriage ended dramatically. Practically overnight my world shattered. Everything I had identified with was gone and in its place was a dark hole I dared not look into. With time, I pieced my life together admirably. But when I was alone, a black mass of fear threatened to overwhelm me. Eventually I had to face the fact that the pain of my childhood abandonment – which had haunted me ever since I could remember – was knocking on the door again. Only this time it was much louder! And so instead of running away from it yet again, I decided to make friends with it.

With nothing to lose I realized I might as well relax deeply into the pain. The more I gave in to it, the more my fear softened and eventually the scared victim dissolved into the

Conscious surrender to
what is is the only way to surf the
razor's edge to freedom.

ocean of my being. In the vast spaciousness of *this* moment, I was totally at one with myself and with Life. What had seemed so terrible turned out to be one of my most profound spiritual lessons. It's a lesson I still have to keep applying to other areas of my life but it's not as scary as it used to be.

So you see, pain is God's cosmic joke! So many of us resist pain because we think it is not part of God's plan: how could Our Father allow us to suffer? But the fact is, whenever you experience pain, you can be sure this is a gateway to God. I am reminded of the Indian saint, Neem Keroli Baba who, when faced with people who complained to him about their personal hardship and pain, would respond with: "I love suffering ... it always brings me closer to God!"

When you embrace pain fully with the breadth of your openness and the depth of your presence, you awaken to your true nature. The heart is the bridge between personal and universal consciousness. And so every time you open your heart a little wider because you choose to soften rather than tighten, you dissolve another layer of conditioning that prevents you from seeing the truth of your essential nature. Each time you choose love, you grow spiritually. This is the only true way to liberate yourself from suffering.

The interesting thing is, once you truly commit to spiritual growth you will undoubtedly meet your greatest challenges. In other words, there's no avoiding the pain. So beware, once you step onto the path of awakening there is really no going back! Each challenge will take you to a new edge of resistance which demands that you soften a little more. And this keeps happening over and over again until softening becomes your nature, until all division into pain and pleasure disappears and you finally merge with Divine Oneness.

Awakening to Love and Truth

As you open wider to let Life in, every part of you and your life that is not already held in love will be brought into the light of consciousness to be seen. As you commit to conscious surrender, you will encounter all the hard edges that you normally kick against. Maybe it's the entanglement of relationships or the black pit of financial insecurity. Maybe it's the ugliness of addiction or the niggling desperation of an unfulfilled career. Whatever it is, you can choose to recoil in horror. Or you can choose to hold it tenderly in your heart, just *as it is*. The first choice keeps you trapped. The second choice liberates you.

I watched a movie about the spiritual teacher Ram Dass's life recently and I was really struck by how he has allowed his misfortune to become his healing. In the midst of an active life traveling and teaching he suffered a stroke that left him paralyzed on one side, wheelchair-bound and with a speech impediment. He could have easily retracted into Poor Me; he could have become bitter and railed against Life and God. But instead he opened his heart even wider to accommodate his pain, his confusion, his betrayal, his fear and his helplessness. He'd spent years denying the needs of his body in order to dwell in "higher consciousness" and now

The heart is the bridge between personal and universal consciousness.

he had the courage to confront and ultimately embrace the reality of his mortality.

By opening his heart to his experience just *as it is*, he has not only healed his wounded relationship to his own body but he has also been blessed with a deep silence that permeates every moment of his life. Today, he is happier, wiser, more whole and more peaceful than he has ever been. And, to me, he seems a much more powerful teacher because of it.

The bowl of your heart is much bigger than you think. In fact, it has the capacity to hold the totality of life's experience. In this bowl there's enough space for all the beauty – and all the horror – in the world. Love does not deny anyone or anything access to the milk of human kindness, no matter their actions. In the unbounded spaciousness of an open heart, love is non-judgmental and unconditional.

Love is that which does not change. And that which does not change is your true nature. The deeper you go into love, the clearer you see who you really are. Mostly what we see is colored by our likes and dislikes. The canvas of our reality is formed from childhood patterns. We learn harsh lessons about how life is and then we galvanize them into *good* and *bad*. But each time we contract because we can't bear to feel the full depth of our pain, we avoid looking life straight in the eye. With time, our vision gets distorted. Getting caught up in judgment and labeling means we see the world through the myopic lens of *me*-centered thinking. Sadly, it only serves to keep us small, separate and very lonely.

The bare truth is revealed only when we see with the eyes of the heart. It means seeing things as they are. No frills, no adjustments ... just stark naked awareness. Truth is the direct experience of *what is*.

Truth is the penetration of *this* moment with the depth of your presence. It's what happens when you are rooted in *now*. Opening to life means being truthful to yourself about how you *really* feel. Only by admitting the depth of your suffering can you move beyond it, not by side-stepping it but by going *through* it. The more you open to Life, the deeper your experience. And the closer you get to the truth of who you are.

The truth is that you are deeper than you can imagine and vaster than your wildest dreams. Truth is like a sword that cuts through all ego-constructions to reveal the full splendor of your essential nature. In cutting through all that is false, you are left with the absolute emptiness of Being that is your crowning glory. The truth is that who you *think* you are does not exist. Only the infinite silence of your consciousness is real. In the deep truth of silent awareness you discover you are God. Because, in *this* moment, *God is all there is.*

Making Love with Existence

Love and Truth are like two lovers whose cosmic embrace gives birth to Life over and over again. At the beginning of Creation, when Existence emerged out of Nothingness, the Big Bang created such a rupture that the One divided into two and became *yin* and *yang,* the essential feminine and masculine energies. Everything that exists is a manifestation of *yin* and *yang* coming together in the desire for wholeness. Life would not be possible without this beautiful dance. Another way of saying this is that God – the Source of All That Is – is made manifest through the receptive feminine quality of *being* or Love and the penetrating masculine quality of *presence* or Truth.

Everything that is natural – or true to its nature – is an expression of these two energies. Think of a lion … Have you ever seen a lion give himself a hard time for not being good enough? A lion is always unashamedly a lion, always totally present in *this* and every moment of stalking prey, tearing into flesh, roaring his dominion or snoozing in satiated satisfaction.

Or think of a flower ... A flower offers its presence in each and every moment as the beauty of bold color and intoxicating fragrance. A lion or a flower has no sense of *me* and *mine*. It is neither divided within itself nor at war with the rest of life. Nature is always in a state of wholeness. There's a lot to learn by simply observing the nature of animals and plants.

Nature, however, is not conscious of itself and so lacks the dimensionality of *breadth* and *depth*. Nature simply is. Only we humans have the ability to open wide or just a fraction. Only we are able to penetrate really deep or just dip in our toe. Only we have the power of transformation, the ability to shift our consciousness from the personal to the universal realm. And therefore only we have the opportunity to recognize ourselves as manifestations of God.

In our natural state of full divinity, we humans are the full embodiment of Love and Truth. But the linear trajectory of civilization pulls us away from our center, warping our love and distorting our truth. Mostly we respond to life with self-justified fear rather than risk the openness of love and we choose to hide behind our lies rather than face the piercing truth. Cut off from both our own nature and the natural world, Love and Truth are having a hard time reuniting in Divine Oneness.

The rift between feminine and masculine is a wound that is carried in the heart of every human being. Internally, we experience it as the conflict between our inner female and inner male. Do we trust the flow of our intuition or do we allow the sharpness of our intellect to rule? Should we nurture our family and friends or should we carve out a career? Externally, we see it most clearly in the battle of the sexes and especially within intimate relationship. We also see it in the limiting gender roles of society, the conflict between science and mysticism, and the separation of Heaven and Earth. The male-female wound is ultimately an expression of the separation from God. It seems that the further away we move from our true nature, the more we suffer.

I believe we can heal this separation by consciously embodying the full *openness* of our feminine energy and the full *depth* of our masculine energy, thereby unlocking the

Love is that which does not change.
And that which does not change is
your true nature.

spiritual power of our essential nature. The meeting of Love
and Truth is an alchemical marriage that takes place within
each one of us and has the power of personal and global
transformation. By awakening to Love and Truth in *every*
moment and *every* aspect of our lives, we come into *right*
relationship with ourselves, with those around us, with the
planet and with every part of our lives. And in opening wide
to receive Life *as it is now* and penetrating deep into *this*
moment, we make love with Existence.

Existence demands that we soften into her, that we relax
and open our hearts. Whether we hear this demand or not
is another matter because, most often, she whispers and
we miss the call amidst our cries of *me, me, me!* Sometimes
she shouts, hoping we will hear, like when illness strikes
unexpectedly or the thing we cherish most is suddenly taken
away from us. If we are wide awake, we will hear the call

and be drawn irresistibly closer just like a lover drawn to his beloved. Indeed, Existence *is* the Beloved who forever beckons us to abandon ourselves to the moment.

In deep surrender, all illusions fall away; all *me*-centered thinking and self-protective actions are left behind. In their place is a vast spacious unbounded joy and a deep intimacy with Life. When we keep softening and opening through all of life's experiences – from the mundane to the transcendent and from the delightful to the terrible – then every experience takes us into the arms of God.

And in this moment, we re-create ourselves in God's image. And Heaven and Earth are reunited once again.

Chapter 2

THE JOURNEY OF TRANSFORMATION

We do not have to trek all the way to the Himalayas to find God. And neither do we need to turn away from everyday life. But we do need to make the one from our heads to our hearts.

In order to awaken to our true nature, we need to put on the brakes and change direction. Firstly, we need to slow down and ask ourselves: "What am I really looking for?" Secondly, rather than getting carried along with every thought and desire that pops into our minds, we can wait for a moment and ask ourselves: "Is this what I really want?"

We may think that yet another box of chocolates or pair of shoes will make us happy, or that chatting long hours with friends on the phone will make us feel connected, or that working hard to step up the career ladder will make us more empowered. But most of the time, these are distractions that prevent us from truly getting to know ourselves. I've noticed how the times I am tempted to reach out for something I think I need are the times I am not wanting to stop and face my discomfort.

When we look outside of ourselves for something to make us feel complete, we never get to know the fullness of our own true nature.

From Horizontal to Vertical

Most of us live in a *horizontal* reality in which we seek to get love, power, self-worth, wealth, happiness – or whatever else we think we need – from the external world. This reality is where the ego lives. And since the ego sees everything in terms of gain and loss, we try to get as much as we can for *me* and *mine* from other people, from the world, from Life and from God.

In a horizontal reality, we create unconscious transactions with our family, friends and lovers just so we can feel better. Here are some of the unspoken contracts we make: "I need you to stay with me so that I feel loved;" "I need you to agree with me so that I feel powerful;" "I need you to be nice to me so that I feel good enough." Do you recognize any of these? When it comes to the world, we accumulate status, money and consumer products in order to make ourselves feel more complete: "I need that qualification so that I can feel strong;" "I need more money so that I can feel worthy;" "I need more things so that I can feel abundant." When it comes to life, we squeeze in as much fun and pleasure as we can lest it pass us by and we die unfulfilled. And when it comes to God, we pray that He gives us what we want so that we don't have to dive too deeply into our pain.

Living within a horizontal reality means you are run ragged by your ego as it looks this way and that way to protect *me* and *mine*. The thing is, however much love, money or status you try to grab from the external world, none of it will ever fill the hole you feel inside. The love, power, worth, and wealth you seek are actually found within.

The journey of awakening requires us to just stand still

for a moment. Allowing consciousness to rest easy in *this* moment means that our gaze turns inwards and we begin to see with the eyes of the heart. With practice, our habitual patterns and addiction to *me* and *mine* lose their urgency and new possibilities reveal themselves. When we make the journey from our heads to our hearts, we become aligned with a *vertical* reality in which the illusion of ego dissolves.

In a vertical reality, there is no separation between *me* and *you* or between *me* and *the world*. Here, there is only the eternal flow of *all that is*: you, me, everyone and everything that exists is a manifestation of the One and we are all fed by Source. This is where we find true love, true power, true worth, and true wealth. The real treasure that we seek is that which cannot be gained or lost. And the only thing that you can neither gain nor lose is the jewel of your eternal nature, the essence of your being.

Living in a vertical reality doesn't mean that we become either ascetics or hermits. We don't need to deny ourselves the luxuries in life nor isolate ourselves from human relationships. What living in a vertical reality means is that we can enjoy the full breadth and depth of Life as it is happening without tightening around our fears or clinging to our hopes.

Far from being dry and boring, life in the vertical reality is rich and delightful!

Total Spiritual Revolution

Many of us equate the journey of awakening with "becoming spiritual." It's as if we add spirituality to our shopping list, along with a big house, a perfect relationship and an easy life. But true spirituality is not a commodity: it is not something we can buy in order to make our lives better.

So often in today's world, becoming spiritual means doing spiritual things. The point we seem to miss is that without

The real treasure that we seek is that which cannot be gained or lost. And the only thing that you can neither gain nor lose is the jewel of your eternal nature, the essence of your being.

truly turning our attention inside, all the yoga, chanting and positive affirmations in the world cannot transform our consciousness. Spiritual materialism pervades modern culture and plays havoc with our egos. Chogyam Trungpa, the Tibetan Buddhist teacher known for his crazy wisdom, described it as creating a beautiful junk shop: we keep collecting information, knowledge and methods from this philosophy and that path until we reassure ourselves that we are spiritual, but all we end up with is a room full of handed-down knowledge that is yet another "display ... of the grandiose quality of ego." It's easy for the ego that serves to protect small self at all costs to shed one disguise for another. An ego masquerading as a "spiritual self" is one of the most common pitfalls on the path of personal development and one that seems particularly easy for our power-crazed culture to fall for.

The thing is, however many trees you hug and however many spiritual books you read, unless you burn with the desire for Love and Truth, you will just be fooling yourself. So often, being spiritual only serves to create more separation. For example, on a recent trip to India, I spent some time living in close proximity to a group of Westerners. One of the women impressed everyone with her stories of the gurus she had met and spiritual disciplines she had tried. She was more than happy to share her experiences at any given opportunity and most people were more than happy to listen. But as the days and weeks passed, she demanded more and more attention and became increasingly judgmental of anyone who didn't agree with her, to the point of being mentally and emotionally abusive.

It was clear to me that this woman had created such a strong identity out of her "spiritual self" that she had built an insurmountable wall between herself and every other human being. Behind her spiritual façade, I saw a very lonely and scared little girl. Not only had she placed "the enlightened ones" on a pedestal but she had also placed "the rest of humanity" in the gutter. Unfortunately, she was left stranded somewhere in between.

It takes courage and honesty to penetrate the veil of illusion by jumping from doing spiritual things to a place of deep surrender. Only by diving deep into the mystery of Life can the spell of separation be broken. Only by total embrace of your experience in *this* moment can real transformation happen. It doesn't matter whether you are

No amount of fighting to save the whales or singing for world peace will ultimately create harmonious humanity if we are still divided within. If you have not fully embraced yourself then how can you fully embrace the world?

meditating in a golden temple or immersed in the hustle and bustle of a shopping mall ... every circumstance provides the opportunity for awakening.

The journey of going inside is an absolute prerequisite to any change in our external circumstances. So often we try to fix the world before we have taken an honest look at what is going on inside ourselves. We believe that doing good deeds or campaigning for social change will make the world a better place. But the truth is that this doesn't work in the long run. No amount of fighting to save the whales or singing for world peace will ultimately create a harmonious humanity if we are still divided within. If you have not fully embraced yourself then how can you fully embrace the world? Love and Truth are the only things that will heal the world, not more fighting or more division into right versus wrong. If you cannot dive deep inside and soften into your own pain, then you cannot truly love the world.

We project those aspects of ourselves that we label *unacceptable* or *wrong* or *bad*, onto the world, and then in turn label *them* as *unacceptable* or *wrong* or *bad* to the same degree that we hide them from ourselves. The world is as we perceive it. If you believe you are unlovable, you will behave in ways that are unloving towards yourself and so you will experience the world as an unloving place. If you believe that humans are inherently selfish creatures, you will seek to protect yourself from others and so you will experience the world as a selfish place. If you believe that God is vengeful, you will try to always "get it right" so that you protect yourself from his wrath, and you will experience life as a punishing place. Your core beliefs about yourself, others, the world, life and God create your reality. And humanity's collective beliefs create the world we live in. Today's world of violence, greed and alienation is a reflection of the fear-based platform most of us operate from. The world of political, economic and religious division we see is simply a reflection of how divided we are within.

Only by turning within can consciousness transform. This is the key to a real transformation of both our inner and outer worlds. Consciousness needs to make a revolution – a turning around and turning within – in order for personal and global change to happen. Only by transformation of consciousness can there be a total spiritual revolution. When each of us takes full responsibility for our own inner reality then a real change in the world around us becomes a possibility.

When each of us takes full responsibility for our own inner reality then a real change in the world around us becomes a possibility. Only by transformation of consciousness can there be a total spiritual revolution.

A Holographic Universe

Much of humanity's history has been clouded by a veil that has kept inner and outer realities separate from each other. This is still true today. For the vast majority of people, the external quality of their lives is disconnected from their internal condition, and the global state of affairs has nothing to do with their state of consciousness. Ever since Newton proclaimed that the universe functions as a gigantic machine according to strict laws of cause and effect, we humans have been excluded from the overall equation. It's a cold and lonely world in which our only purpose is to stand outside of life as helpless onlookers.

But this traditional worldview, in which matter and energy (or consciousness) are separate entities, no longer makes sense in the light of ground-breaking new discoveries in fields such as quantum physics, holistic medicine, neurophysiology and consciousness research. The current view is that far from being linear and mechanistic reality is, in fact, *fluid* and *holographic*. Today's leading-edge scientists are coming to the same conclusion as mystics have throughout the ages: that Existence is made up of a unified web of energy, everything is interconnected, and there is no separation between inner and outer worlds. To put it another way, consciousness and matter are totally interdependent and our reality is created from this interaction.

In a holographic universe you can zoom in on any part and find an accurate representation of the whole. It's a view that agrees with the ancient wisdom of "the microcosm contains the macrocosm" or "as above, so below." Examples of the holographic nature of Existence can be found wherever the world of matter and the world of energy interface. We can see it in the correlation between Nature's cycles and the human life cycle and we can see it in the relationship between planetary placements at birth and the expression of an individual's psyche. And we can also see it in the evolutionary development of consciousness in the animal kingdom that mirrors the biology of the human brain.

This holographic mapping reminds me of looking at fractal geometry where zooming in just keeps on revealing the pattern within the pattern and always revealing the whole. William Blake expressed this most eloquently when he said: "To see a world in a grain of sand, and heaven in a wild flower, to hold infinity in the palm of your hand, and eternity in an hour."

Even though mass consciousness is caught up in the conventional Newtonian world, the collective reality paradigm has been slowly shifting over recent years. As more and more people become spiritual seekers, experiment with psychotropics, and discover new realities through personal transformation tools, so do the boundaries between inner and outer become more permeable. Even though the world appears to function as it has always done, there is a wave of consciousness change currently sweeping across the planet.

If you are reading this book now, you too are part of this wave of change.

A Map of Consciousness

I remember as a child I would often sit in a kind of rapture. Oblivious to what was going on around me, I enjoyed a bliss-like state that I can only now describe as "coming home". This experience of "coming home" is, in fact, the journey consciousness makes to return to Source. It is the journey from horizontal to vertical reality. And it is one that we can choose to make in every moment.

In order to understand how consciousness makes this journey and how this relates to personal and global transformation, I have put together a map that draws together both science and spirituality. In this map there are three levels of reality, each one having an inner dimension (how we perceive the world) and an outer dimension (the world that is collectively created).

The first level of reality – the one that we are most familiar with – is the *personal* realm. In the world of science this is the *material* world, the world of objects and events. This is the world of form that operates according to cause and effect. Here, particles travel slower than the speed of light therefore objects appear as separate solid entities and events follow each other sequentially. This material realm corresponds to ordinary everyday consciousness where we perceive time as linear and space as three-dimensional.

Small mind lives here, thinking in terms of past and future, separating *me* from *you*, and generally clinging to what it knows. The name of the game here is self-preservation, security and survival. Necessary perhaps when crossing the road, but not in giving life its depth and meaning. When we operate solely on this level, we remain victims of our circumstances. Life is *good* or *bad* depending on whether we like or dislike what is happening. This is the world of duality, the horizontal reality in which we see the external world as a place to get what we think we need to sustain us. At this level, we are stuck in the spell of separation.

On a collective level, this is the fear-based world of racism, terrorism and environmental pollution that we currently live in. It's a world in which religion divides nations, most of the world's finances are poured into military development, and the chasm between rich and poor is growing out of control. Just like our internal world, the external world operates in a horizontal reality: we compete with each other to get what we can, we dominate each other to feel more powerful and we fight each other to protect what we have. In this world of win or lose, the end result can only be destruction.

The next level of reality is the *transition* realm. In physics this is the *quantum* world, where cause and effect are fluid and only probabilities can be measured. Here, waves and particles are interchangeable and everything travels at the same speed as light. In this "in-between" zone, form arises out of the subtle, vibrating quantum field. In other words, matter is created from energy.

This is where the visible and invisible worlds converge, where thoughts, emotions and intuition collide with the physical. This is the world of imagination where we create our reality for better or for worse. It's the place where prayer, faith and intention create miracles, where synchronicities happen and where we are inspired by a flash of creative genius. It's also the world that shamans have journeyed to for millennia to call for healing and where New Age seekers travel for higher guidance.

The *transition* realm is the point at which consciousness takes a pause and turns away from the world of external form. In the space between *this* and *that*, the journey of transformation begins. As consciousness travels inwards, you get to see how your external world is a mirror of your internal world. Now, you are no longer a victim but a co-creator of life, a manifestor of your own destiny. Here, every event of your life – however big or small and however blissful or painful – has meaning because you recognize your role in its creation.

Many spiritual seekers stop here, believing that they have reached the end of the road. It's not surprising since the gifts are great and the feeling of empowerment can be enough to last a lifetime. But the journey is incomplete. Only the final step into the *universal* realm will take you all the way home. In the world of physics this is the *virtual* world, the formless world beyond the speed of light. Here, there is no time and no space, just pure infinite creative potential. This realm has been called the Zero Point Field and, far from being empty, it is an invisible universal field of virtual energy that seems to contain the blueprint for perfect form. Every single thing that exists arises from this place, moves towards the quantum realm where it becomes manifest and ends up in the material realm as form. The Zero Point Field is immeasurable, unbounded and omnipresent. It exists in infinite quantity and so can never be exhausted. Science has been investigating this as a potential source for unlimited free energy. Spirituality calls it the transcendent realm of pure consciousness, Prana, the Breath of God, the Holy Spirit.

This is the vertical reality where all boundaries dissolve and consciousness merges with the oneness of *all that is*. When you arrive here, you recognize your Budhha-nature, that part of you that is eternal and true. And you recognize that Buddha-nature is in everyone and everything, it is the ground from which Existence springs. A humanity that operates from a deep understanding that *we are all one* creates a living Buddha-field that has the capacity to transform mass consciousness to a higher level.

Going all the way from horizontal to vertical is the only way to find God. Like so many spiritual seekers, I spent many years trying out different spiritual disciplines. Each time I thought I'd "got it:" I'd found happiness or freedom or peace. But each time, after the honeymoon period, I'd be just as miserable as before. It was only when I finally gave up trying to be spiritual – when I stopped hanging onto the highs and avoiding the lows – that real transformation happened. When I finally let go into the vastness of Life with all its ups and downs I found the stillness I'd been looking for.

If you truly look deep inside, you will arrive at the untarnished Truth of silent Being. In deep surrender, consciousness always returns to Source and rests eternally in unbounded Love.

Awakening to Love and Truth in *every* moment and in *every* place is the only way to transform yourself and the world around you.

Zorba the Buddha

Everything that exists is a gateway to the divine. Whether you see life as a dangerous place full of dark corners, hard edges and harsh lessons or whether you behold the Beloved in everything that happens depends on how deeply you have dived into the nature of your own being. The most mundane act becomes a sacred experience when you hold it tenderly in love and open deeply to its truth in *this* moment.

Admittedly, it's easy to get caught in the spell of separation whilst raising a family, making money to make ends meet, pursuing a career or campaigning for justice. The trouble and strife of everyday life is a great place to hide behind a mountain of storylines. In the midst of "I'm doing the best for my children," and "I have to take care of my future," there's no time to look for God! Getting involved in ordinary human living is traditionally viewed as a distraction from the spiritual path. But, whilst this may have been true

Going all the way, from horizontal to vertical, is the only way to find God.

several hundred years ago, it is no longer enough to retreat into a cave and contemplate life from afar.

Denial of earthly life simply widens the gap between human experience and divine expression. Only by embracing everything can the separation be healed. You can awaken to Love even through all the challenges, difficulties, hurdles and heartbreaks of being human. You can open to Truth even in the midst of the business of human "comings and goings." God lives right here and now, not "out there" somewhere. And since you – like me – probably find yourself in the midst of the high-speed modern world, then this is your doorway to God!

Only by embracing fully both the pleasure and the pain of being a 21st-century human can consciousness evolve to the next level. In the Western world we have more material comforts than we have ever known, more opportunities to grow than in previous generations and more freedom to explore ourselves and the world around us. We don't need to deny ourselves the privileges of modern life but neither should we overlook the riches offered by diving into the depths of our hearts. The new consciousness is a meeting of inner and outer worlds. It's the journey of going inside to find Love and Truth as well as enjoying the fruits of our material world. Having a deep passion for life in all its manifestations whilst being able to see beyond the surface reality of the material means you can "be in the world but not of it." When you can embrace both your human and divine nature, then you can celebrate your totality and say a big "Yes!" to Life!

The enlightened mystic and 21st-century visionary, Osho, had a great name for the new human being that is evolving: *Zorba the Buddha*. *Zorba the Buddha* is both passionate and transcendent. He (or she) enjoys earthly pleasures whilst not being attached to them. He goes out into the world to work, play and create as well as going inside to develop spiritual awareness. He is fully present in his body whilst knowing that his true essence is Buddha-nature. He lives consciously, awake in Love and Truth in every aspect of life, from food to sex, from work to money, from relationship to environment. Becoming a *Zorba the Buddha* means you are a fully integrated human being who lives in harmony with the world and sees God in everyone and everything.

*God lives right **here** and **now**, not "out there" somewhere.*

When each of us becomes a *Zorba the Buddha*, the world will truly change. We will no longer be spiritual seekers doing spiritual things. Instead, the fragrance of our true spiritual nature will permeate our lives in every way. Whether we are washing dishes, cooking a meal, playing with our children or making love, every circumstance can be a sacred moment. You do not have to pray for Love, for when you have embraced your true nature you realize that *love is who you are*. And neither do you have to search for Truth, for when you rest deeply inside *this* moment, you see that *truth is all there is*.

When we fully embody the openness of our Love-nature and the depth of our Truth-nature, we will give birth to a new world in which there is no separation between the material and the spiritual and there is no conflict between human and divine. In this new world, Love will be expressed by caring for ourselves, for each other and for the planet that is our home. And Truth will be the expression of our open hearts.

Each and every one of us can realize our divine nature and become a *Zorba the Buddha* right here and now. This is the new path of conscious living that has the power to transform our inner and outer worlds.

Right Relationship

To live consciously is to be in *right relationship* with every aspect of your life. We tend to think that relationship is something we have, something that we fit into our lives in order to get security or love or pleasure. But this is not true: Life *is* relationship. We are actually in relationship with Life all the time. We interact with our friends, our families, our lovers and everyone we meet whether it is in the office, the supermarket or on the bus. We interact with our day-to-day work, our creativity and our life's purpose. We interact with money, society and the world. Every day we interact with our food, our environment and all the resources we make use of. In every moment we are interacting with our bodies, our feelings and our thoughts. There is not a single thing that exists that we are not in relationship with.

The issues we have in a personal one-to-one relationship are the same as the issues we have in life. If we cannot surrender to the process of relationship, then we cannot surrender to the process of Life. And vice versa. It doesn't matter what form our relationship or our life takes. It doesn't matter what the details are, whether it is successful or a failure, whether we are rich or poor, or even whether we are happy or sad. What *does* matter is how *total* we are, whether we give ourselves up completely to Life and trust it to carry us to wherever we are meant to be going. Totality leads to intimacy and intimacy leads to right relationship.

The question is not "how can I fit relationship into my life?" but "how can I get more intimate with Life?" Intimacy with Life means shedding our masks, dropping our defenses, cutting through our storylines. It means becoming a lover of *what is.*

When loving *what is* becomes more important than self-preservation, then you can be sure you are on the way to finding God.

Gateways to God

In order to explore how to live consciously, I have identified seven aspects of Life ranging from the physical to the transcendental. Each one of these is a gateway to God. Each gateway is shrouded by a veil that gives the illusion of separation when viewed from the personal realm: this is the samsara of the horizontal reality. But when your perspective shifts to the universal, the secret hidden within each gateway is revealed. As you awaken to Love and Truth, each veil dissolves and you find yourself floating freely in the vertical reality. It's as if you wake up from a dream and see that God is *right here* where you are!

The first gateway is the Body. It's so available to us that it's easy to overlook this one. Because it is so dense and apparently solid, we very often forget that our physical form is a direct doorway to the subtle realms of the divine. The second gateway is the Mind. Here, the doorway to God is found by entering the gap between thoughts and by letting go into the timeless zone of the eternal *now*. The third gateway is the Self and includes on a surface level the personality as well as the whole array of our emotions, and on a deeper level the patterns revealed by our soul's unique journey. The fourth gateway of Relationship – and here I mean the place in which we meet another human being – is perhaps the one that holds the most potent possibility for transformation in today's world. It is here that the struggle of human love can be transformed to the blessing of divine love.

*When loving **what is** becomes more important than self-preservation, then you can be sure you are on the way to finding God.*

Now we move beyond the sphere of the individual and into the collective realm. The fifth gateway is the World, which includes the mass of humanity, the systems created by society such as politics, economics and media, the work you do, creativity and money. Beyond the world and its human affairs is the world of Nature. This is the sixth gateway of the Planet and includes all living creatures that run, swim, fly and crawl, all green things that grow towards the light, all mountains, rocks, rivers and seas, as well as the natural elemental forces of sun, wind, water and earth. And finally, the seventh gateway is Spirit. This is the transcendent realm of the divine that has been hidden behind the dusty veil of religion for thousands of years. This one holds the final key to understanding that God is in everything and everywhere and points the way to the new vertical paradigm that is emerging today.

These seven gateways are explored in depth in Part II. As you step through each gateway you will discover the secret that has the power to transform your world. Instead of looking outside of yourself for salvation, you will awaken to your true nature and become that which you seek.

There's a wonderful story told by Osho that sums it up perfectly. It goes something like this. When God created the world, he lived on the earth. But he was hassled by the incessant demands of people who each wanted their desires met. God asked his council what he should do to escape these increasing demands and they suggested he hide in a remote place high in the Himalayas. But God responded that eventually he would be found by those who conquer mountains. Someone suggested he hide on the moon, but God responded that one day man would reach the moon too. Someone else suggested he hide in the stars, but God responded that even there he would eventually be found. Finally someone whispered in God's ear and God rejoiced: "Yes I will hide in the only place where man will never look – in man himself!" And this is where God has been hiding ever since.

God is much closer than you think. He is in the fabric of your bones, the beating of your heart, the vibration of your voice, the intimacy of your breath. All you have to do is look inside.

PART II:

The Seven Gateways

Chapter 3

EMBODYING THE DIVINE:
The Gateway of the Body

The greatest gift you have ever been given is your body. Whatever shape it comes in – however perfect or imperfect – your body is a wondrous doorway to the divine.

Not only does your body hold the miracle of Life but it also holds the secrets of the Universe. Right here, in the tangible world of flesh and blood, is everything you need to know about the transcendent world of spirit. Your body is a microcosm of Existence: just as the three-dimensional world of matter contains a unified energy field of infinite proportions, so does your body contain the invisible and indivisible world of consciousness. Quantum physics tells us that every solid particle is composed of more than 99.99 percent empty space and that this space is actually intensely alive with the unmanifest power of creation. In the same way, when we look closely, our bodies are made up of a vast field of quantum intelligence that is the source of our aliveness.

Tapping into this innate intelligence is not only the key to unbounded health but also the doorway to abiding truth. Bringing the depth of your presence and the breadth of your openness right into the density of physical form reveals the underlying reality of your limitless nature. It's a beautiful paradox that the deeper you go into the world of form, the closer you get to the formless.

When you fully inhabit your body with your consciousness, there is a dissolution of boundaries that transports you from

---

It's a beautiful paradox that the deeper you go into the world of form, the closer you get to the formless.

a space-time location to the dimensionless zone of Being. Inside every twitch of your muscles, every tremor of your skin, every beat of your heart and every whisper of your breath, is the key to ecstatic liberation. What we seek is not so far away: it is *right here* with us at all times.

It is so easy to take our physical form for granted that we forget that God lives very close by.

Attuning to the Cosmic Flow

The body is an exquisite sensory organism, able to detect the slightest fluctuation in sensation. In bringing the full depth of our presence into the subtleties of feeling that live inside our form, we experience the effervescent aliveness of our deeper quantum nature. And it is here in the quantum realm – where body and mind interface – that we choose to either open up to receive the full flow of Existence or close down to allow only a trickle of life-energy to reach us.

In closing down against the fullness of *this* moment, we deny ourselves access to an intelligent power that holds all the information we need for perfect health and harmony.

Denial of *what is* means we can hide behind poor eating habits, food addictions and sedentariness. Poor Me loves to slip into entropy, blaming it on the inevitability of the biological process. The high incidence of degenerative diseases in the West – such as osteoarthritis, heart disease and cancer – has more to do with our victimhood than with our physiological function. Contrary to what the majority of the medical profession would have us believe, these diseases are not caused by natural wear and tear but are the result of self-sabotaging lifestyle habits.

Even when we think we're being "health-conscious", we're often out of alignment with the cosmic flow that's the source of radiant well-being. I recently read Jane Fonda's autobiography in which she chronicles her transformation from a neurotic young girl totally out of touch with her body to a vibrant woman of nearly 70 who has learned to love and respect every aspect of her physical nature. What resonated with me most was her meteoric rise to fame in the early 1980s as an aerobics instructor. At the time she was my heroine and I emulated her every move. But like her, I realize now that I was just using control to cover up the hollow place between my body and my soul.

Strict dietary and exercise regimes are mostly a product of a horizontal perspective on health. However many vitamin pills we pop and however toned our muscles, our body remains starved of that which truly nourishes it. A body without the light of consciousness and without the radiance of love is no more than an inert lump of clay. It's a mechanistic view in which we lose our connection to the sacredness of our inner nature.

By bringing our awareness to rest in the vibrating energy field that lives within, we shift into alignment with the vertical. Now the body becomes less like a machine and more like a musical instrument. A perfectly tuned instrument offers no resistance to the vibrational dance of particles that creates sonic harmony. In the same way, a body attuned to the cosmic flow offers no resistance to whatever is happening in *this* moment: it is in perfect harmony with the rhythm of life. In the horizontal realm we are disconnected from Source and we struggle to stay astride the ever-changing tides of Life. But in the vertical dimension we are nourished by the endless flow of *all that is* and we have an implicit trust in the natural cycles of both our inner and outer worlds.

In the horizontal, we are inflexible: we attempt to control

both the details of our lives as well as the performance of our bodies. But in the vertical, we are fluid: life is effortless and our bodily function is poetry in motion. How we move our bodies is how we move through life. Whether we do yoga, running, skating or swimming, exercising just to whip ourselves into shape so that we look good or to prove that we're the strongest or the fastest keeps us fragmented. When body, mind and spirit do not function as one harmonious whole, we run on "borrowed energy" and eventually we become depleted. I understand now why I spent so much of my youth in a state of fatigue even though I was technically very fit!

The recognition of the body as a doorway to the divine means we honor it as a vehicle for our soul's unique expression. When we make conscious lifestyle choices, all our bodies – physical, emotional, mental and spiritual – come into harmonious alignment. In a state of unity, every movement – from lifting a tea cup to the most advanced yoga asana – is filled with the presence and love of Existence. The movement of your body as well as the movement of your life become not something that you *do* but something that is done *through* you. It's a subtle shift in perception from the goal-oriented view of the horizontal to the moment-to-moment appreciation of the vertical. In expanding our perspective to include our multi-dimensional nature, we move from being victims of biology to being co-creators of a state of "higher health" in which peace, joy and fulfillment prevail. Through the power of conscious surrender, you are filled with cosmic energy from Source and your body becomes an ecstatic vessel of the divine.

Meeting the Stories Held in the Body

Your body is a holographic map of how you think, feel and move through life. Every bump and lump, every contour and groove, is a story untold. You may spend a lifetime running away from what you are too scared to meet in the naked fullness of your awareness ... but the body never lies.

Every feeling that is ignored gets lodged in the body as tension. Every emotion that remains unresolved gets locked in as pain. And every self-defeating thought of limitation gets recorded as weakness. Failing to meet life with the totality of our being means our reluctance translates into physical retraction. Hard belly and shallow breath – over and over again – become an armoring that shields the tenderness of an open heart. And there's nothing like an armored body to prevent us from softening into the delicious depth of our feelings.

A body that has learnt to tighten into fear and shape itself around the shallowness of storylines is guaranteed to get us out of synch with the natural rhythm of Life.

But neither neglect nor control will free us from the inescapable fact that we are bound by physical form and all its imperfections and fluctuations. Only by total acceptance of the full spectrum of human experience as filtered through our senses – from ecstatic pleasure to agonizing pain – can we transcend our density and reach for the light. The body is more than just a complex arrangement of chemicals: it is a bio-spiritual portal into the quantum realm of unlimited potential. It is *right here* in the tangible evidence of our existence that we find that which we truly are.

Sometimes, though, we just refuse to recognize our physical form as a doorway to the most sacred part of ourselves. It's true that nutrition and other lifestyle factors play an important role in the contribution to biological dysfunction. But ultimately, all pain, illness and disease arise from our inability to let go into the tender places that lie beneath the hardness of our storylines. The most common stories are those of resentment, criticism, guilt and unworthiness. As Deepak Chopra tells us, the biochemistry of the body is a product of our beliefs, thoughts and emotions. Every unloving thought we have towards another or towards ourself gets imprinted as a cellular memory that creates biological disharmony.

This was brilliantly depicted in the recent film *What the Bleep Do We Know!?* which brought quantum reality into the public eye. There's one particularly memorable scene in which vivid animated graphics show us how repetitive negative thoughts and emotions create the equivalent of a violent thunderstorm in our brains, sending destructive

The body is more than just a complex arrangement of chemicals: it is a bio-spiritual portal into the quantum realm of unlimited potential.

neurotransmitters coursing around the body and ultimately creating cellular destruction. We're then shown how to undo the damage by sending neuro-chemical messengers of peace, harmony and love.

Pain, illness and disease are always a call from your inner being to pay attention to *this* moment. They're a call to turn your attention inwards and listen to the body's deeper cry for self-acceptance. I've discovered that at the core of all pain, illness and disease is a state of unforgiveness. When we cannot forgive others for what they have done to us nor forgive ourselves for being unlovable, we remain stuck in the past. Judgment means we refuse to grow into the magnificence of our full potential. Only by meeting each layer of emotion as it arises in a non-judgmental space can we dissolve our armoring and shift from the bondage of a past-future orientation to the freedom of presence.

Forgiveness is the willingness to experience the totality of our hurt and then let it go. The power of change is always in the *now*! Forgiveness has the power to heal all pain, illness and disease. I personally know people who have miraculously healed themselves of major illnesses by getting to the root of the emotion that caused it. And I have also experienced it myself with minor ailments that have vanished when I have inquired honestly into what lies beneath.

Every ache and pain, every deviation from optimal health – whether it is a minor illness such as flu or a life-threatening disease such as cancer – is a message from God. Even congenital deformities, hereditary and transmitted diseases are a calling to soften into a deeper embrace of self. Whilst some conditions may not be curable on the physical level, a tremendous amount of healing on the soul level can happen through the power of love. In God's world, there are no accidents: inside every apparent mishap of Nature lies the unfailing gift of transformation. It's never too late to turn inwards and make the journey home to our essential self.

Conscious Eating

Our relationship to food is an intimate one. And it's a wonderfully accurate reflection of our relationship to Life. You can tell a lot about how someone takes in life by watching *what* – and *how* – they eat!

In my 20s, I was obsessed with finding the optimal diet.

I tried a wide variety of regimes ranging from macrobiotics to superfoods to raw food. But none of them worked and I still suffered from digestive problems and low energy levels. It wasn't until many years later that I discovered I'd missed out a vital ingredient: love. The bottom line was that I didn't love myself nor did I love my life. I was so shut down that I was unable to assimilate what Life had to offer. And this was perfectly mirrored by my inability to metabolize what Nature provided for my plate.

Through trial and error, I've learnt that how we digest our food is how we digest life's experiences. When we are aligned to the truth of our inner radiance, our internal fire transmutes everything into goodness. And into godliness. This is perhaps one of the most powerful health secrets! The quality of physical – and soul – nourishment we receive

When we are aligned to the truth of our inner radiance, our internal fire transmutes everything into goodness. And into godliness.

depends on the depth of our presence and the breadth of our openness. It means getting conscious of how we are in every moment. And it especially means getting conscious of how we eat.

Conscious eating is not about imposing a strict dietary regime because you think it's "good for you." Rather it's an on-going inquiry into what is really happening here, a checking in with yourself every time you sit down to eat: "Am I open or closed? Is my belly soft and breath slow or is my belly tight and breath fast? How do I feel after I eat this? What is the effect on my body, mind, emotions? Am I enlivened or sluggish? Am I uplifted or depressed?" By eating consciously, we are more likely to choose a diet that is light, fresh and pure because it helps us become light in body, clear in mind and joyful in spirit.

Conscious eating is an act of love, just as is conscious living. Being gentle and attentive both towards what is on our plate and towards our bodily responses to what we ingest reflects a deep intimacy with the oneness of Life. This sensitivity allows us to see the chain of events that has brought the food to our kitchen, to feel how every aspect of the journey – from seed sown in soil to factory packaging – has an effect on its vibrational quality. Food that arrives on our plates in a peaceful manner, having honored the intricate web of life along the way, grown with love and served with love, will be of a superior quality to food carelessly grown and aggressively produced.

So many diseases common to the West – as well as the physical and psychological symptoms of early ageing – are created by our unconsciousness around food. Unconscious eating is a horizontal experience in which we often reach out for "comfort food" in order to feel better. Mostly we eat too much too fast and too many of the wrong things. I used to stuff myself with food as a way of numbing my feelings, until I realized that I was harming myself by being insensitive to my deeper needs. In slowing down and breathing into the pause before the first bite, we activate the body's innate intelligence. And the body always knows what to eat, when to eat and how much to eat.

It's worth remembering that when we fill ourselves with junk food, our bodies become a dumping ground both for toxic substances and for toxic feelings. Junk food is dense, laden with fats, sugars and artificial additives, as well as mass-produced in less than loving environments. Eventually all this rubbish becomes a sticky mass that blocks our digestive power and obscures our consciousness. Body and mind are inextricably linked. Research shows that the gut functions as a "second brain" with the same biochemistry and neural circuitry.

Loving your body and loving your food goes far beyond "health fads." Food is more than mere calories, vitamins and minerals. It has the capacity to bring us closer to the verticality of our divine nature. As my relationship to Life has changed over the years, so has my relationship to food. As my hunger for God has become my over-riding appetite, so have my choices in what, when and how to eat become easier. Today, I eat very simply yet every mouthful is a delight and I eat less but am more fulfilled than ever.

Whether you are eating a sumptuous meal or a humble sandwich, you can choose to see it as a mere visceral response to hunger or you can open to receive what is truly being offered. By recognizing the unifying force that permeates everything that exists, eating becomes more than a basic survival issue. Instead, it becomes a prayer in action, an honoring of God's bountiful presence. When we see God in everything, we cannot help but be grateful for what springs from Mother Earth's fertile land. Just like us, every fruit, root, grain and seed that grows on our planet is spirit condensed as matter. Every bite we take is an act of communion with an aspect of God.

It is love that feeds that part of us which is beyond mortal flesh. And it is love that allows the radiant glow of well-being to permeate everything we do and everything we are.

Holy Communion of Breath

Even more intimate than our relationship to food is our relationship to our breath. It's probably the most powerful key we have been given for unlocking the gateway of the body.

When we bring our full consciousness to the action of breathing – to the sensation of breath rising and falling – we enter directly into the timelessness of the present moment. Have you noticed how you can't be busy worrying about the past or making plans for the future *and* be aware of your breath at the same time? Breathing consciously is the fastest route to being here *now*!

So often though, we are caught up in our heads and our

breath becomes unconscious. When you tighten with anxiety or contract in fear, your breath also becomes shallow and closed. When we fear taking Life in fully, our breath becomes incomplete. When inhale and exhale do not meet each other as two equals, but instead one is longer or shorter than the other, we set up an internal struggle that reflects our external battle with Existence.

A conscious breath, on the other hand, is a big *"Yes!"* to Life. It's a deep relaxation into all that this moment has to offer. Softening into our breath means we can embrace whatever is happening with love. Soft belly and relaxed breath transcends small-minded likes and dislikes and allows open-hearted OKness with *what is.* So many times I have found myself in situations that have caused me to recoil into the shallowness of my habitual judgments. But I've noticed that the subsequent tightening of my breath creates a subtle yet pervasive sense of nausea that clouds my consciousness and if I just take a few seconds to relax my breath, I immediately return to the lucidity of a non-judgmental heart.

When our in-breath and out-breath meet in relaxed harmony, we complete the cycle of continuity in which giving and receiving flow into each other and become one and the same. The in-breath shows us how we take in Life. It shows us how we welcome in the invisible world of energy and transform it into the molecular world of oxygenation. It is an act of creation in which we are born into the newness of *this* moment. The out-breath shows us how we let go into Life. It shows us how we release back into the unseen world that which has been processed. It is an act of surrender, a death of all that we are in preparation for the rebirth into the next moment.

A complete breath heals the separation between matter and spirit. It's a union that takes place in our hearts, both in metaphysical terms as well as in the tangible language of biology. It is in our hearts that the biochemical conversion of respiration into energy for life takes place and it is in our hearts that we experience the unified wholeness of Being. Every time we breathe, we move beyond form to formlessness. The space between the inhale and the exhale is where we meet God.

The act of breathing is a most intimate one in which, if we bring the full depth of our presence and the full breadth of our openness, we come into right relationship with *all that is.* When we breathe, we take in the same air that has been breathed in and out of every living creature since the beginning of time. Through our breath we are one with all that exists. Breathing is an act of love, a holy communion with Existence itself.

I invite you to take a moment to notice how your breath is right *now.* Are you aware of your breath or are you caught up in your thoughts? Take a moment to sit comfortably and consciously deepen your breath so you become aware of the rise and fall of your chest. Can you feel the sensation of air moving through your nostrils as you inhale and exhale? Keep focusing on your breath ... long, slow, soft inhale. Take in the fullness of *this* moment exactly *as it is,* feel your body open to embrace Life. And when you are as full as you can be,

When we bring our full consciousness to the action of breathing – to the sensation of breath rising and falling – we enter directly into the timelessness of the present moment.

just let go. Let it all out, surrender back into the flow ... long, slow, soft exhale. And allow yourself to relax deeply into *this* moment exactly *as it is*.

Perhaps spend a few minutes doing this with your eyes closed, although it's also OK to keep your eyes open whilst you are reading. Becoming conscious of your breath at all times – whether you are eating, dancing or simply sitting still – is the key to being present. Breath is the common thread that runs through everything that you do and it's a doorway to Being.

Becoming conscious of your breath whilst you go about your day means you are anchored in the unbounded truth of your essential nature whilst still navigating the world of form. It infuses Life with the freshness of unlimited freedom. And puts a lightness into your step!

Entering the Gateway of the Body

And now I invite you to go a little deeper. Bring your attention back to your breath. If you notice any tension in your body, consciously focus on that area and breathe deeply and softly into it. And allow yourself to let go of the tension on the outbreath. Keep doing this until your body feels more relaxed.

Now see if you can become aware of the gap between the in-breath and the out-breath. It's a gentle pause in which nothing happens, just stillness. Can you feel it? Don't try too hard, just be softly aware of it. It's as if you are resting on a cloud ... pause and then allow the inhale or the exhale to happen.

As you keep breathing consciously in this way, you may get a sense of your body becoming lighter or you may feel a subtle vibrating energy running through you. As you relax more deeply, you may get a feeling that your physical boundaries are dissolving. Enjoy this feeling, breathe deeply and softly into it. This is form becoming formless ... you are entering the timeless dimension of inner space!

Breath rising and falling, nothing to do but relax right here and *now*. Enter deep into *this* moment, deep into *this* space. If you become aware of any physical sensation simply move into it more deeply and breathe into it. You may feel your body becoming translucent or you may feel it becoming very expansive. Breathe softly and deeply into this feeling and let yourself fall into the limitless space of *now*. Simply let go into the boundlessness of your inner nature. Enjoy the sensation of being everywhere and nowhere all at the same time ... you are one with *all that is*! Stay in this place for a few more minutes.

Now, very slowly draw your attention back to your physical boundary, breath rising and falling in the center of your chest. Bring your attention to your body sitting, standing or lying down. Feel the sensation of the ground beneath you and feel the solidity of your body. And when you are ready, slowly open your eyes and take in the colors and shapes around you. Now take a deep breath ... you are ready to go about your day. You may notice that you feel much lighter all day. And that events flow more easily for you!

Remember, you can do this by taking "time out" and closing your eyes for a few minutes but you can also do this wherever and whatever you are doing. Every time you become aware of the dimensionless space that resides within, you create space in your life for God to enter. And with more divine presence, you can let go and trust in the goodness of Life!

Chapter 4

ENTERING THE NOW:
The Gateway of Mind

In the 1997 film *Contact* Jodie Foster plays a young scientist obsessed with the search for extra-terrestrial life whilst her human relationships suffer from neglect. In the pivotal scene, she is strapped into a futuristic capsule designed to take her into the far reaches of the Universe. But instead of traveling on a linear trajectory into outer space, she falls down a time-tunnel and travels inwards on a spiraling journey into verticality in which she awakens to a power far greater than that of her own intellect. In the encounter with the ineffable, she is transformed. Gone is the androgynous atheist looking at life through the cold lens of her rational mind. In her place is a woman radiating with the beauty of a heart set alight by God, a woman who finally finds the love she had been misguidedly searching for outside of herself. The outcome of this is that her everyday reality is transformed: from struggle and loneliness to joy and fulfillment.

Likewise, when we too make the choice to step through the gateway of the mind, we leave behind the limitations of linear thinking and enter a majestic universe of awe-inspiring possibilities. In the willingness to search for that which is true, we fall into the gap between thoughts and discover the vastness of Being in which space and time collapse into the eternal *now*.

Here – in this gap – life becomes effortless and you remember that unending peace is your birthright.

Lost in Thinking

Most people are totally unaware that they are lost in thinking. It is calculated that we have an average of 3000 thoughts per day. Even in sleep we are thinking, churning over the day's events, sifting through our fears and desires as they bubble up in the form of dreams. Thinking is undoubtedly the "number one" human preoccupation!

When as a young psychology student I was first introduced to the idea that we could access a state of consciousness that transcended thinking, I was fascinated enough to attend a meditation class. However, after several attempts at sitting silently to "simply watch my thoughts rise and fall like waves on the ocean" I realized that I was completely lost at sea and in danger of drowning! According to my meditation teacher all I had to do was "drop beneath the surface and rest in the vast ocean of consciousness". But as each thought rose and fell, I was caught on the crest of the wave and pulled even further away from any faint possibility of stillness. So intense was my panic every time I became aware of the sheer volume of my thinking that I gave up meditation and didn't return to it for several more years.

Looking back, I see that the feeling of insanity I had experienced was an accurate representation of the state of most of humanity's consciousness. We are so busy following an endless stream of thoughts that we now find ourselves "up the creek without a paddle." If we dare to be still for a moment, we realize we are far away from the wholeness of our innate nature.

The struggle to keep up with incessant thinking is a futile attempt to hold on to that which is essentially impermanent. No sooner does each thought rise to the surface than it slips from our grasp and is replaced by another. In chasing that which is in perpetual motion, we keep the wheel of samsara turning. It's an insane world, in which our outer reality of fear, greed and violence perfectly mirrors our inner reality of fearful, grasping and defensive thinking. Our thoughts tell us we should do this or shouldn't do that, that we need this or want that. There's always one more thing to achieve before we can be happy, one more thing to get before we can be fulfilled. Most of us are so caught up in *doing* and *having* that we have missed the point of being human. We have forgotten how to *be*.

Doing and having are like an itch we cannot scratch. The dream of everlasting satisfaction is always just out of reach but it's never here and *now*! No wonder we're run ragged by stress! Instead, we dwell in the remembrance of what went wrong in the past or we run ahead to make sure it won't go wrong in the future.

Stress is a major contributing factor to physical and mental illness. A person who suffers from high stress levels is twice as likely to develop heart disease. Other conditions linked to stress are cancer, stomach and intestinal disorders, chronic backache and headache, skin problems, anxiety, depression, nervous breakdown and suicide. In a recent study, stress has been shown to dramatically increase the ageing process by speeding up the breakdown of genes inside cells.

Interestingly, it is our *subjective* experience of stress that is the crucial factor. Of course, the modern world is filled with stressful stimuli. City life, especially, has seen over the past two decades an uncomfortable increase in overcrowding, noise pollution, volume of traffic, crime and general aggressiveness. But it is not the external event itself that is the cause of our stress. Rather it is the *story* we create around it. There's a big difference between "My day is ruined," and "I'm sitting in a queue of cars." Or "This is such a pain, I've got better things to do," and "I'm filling in my tax forms." And how about "He's a bastard, he doesn't love me" versus "He left?"

Whether it's the small stuff like traffic jams, noisy children, bills to pay and being late for that all-important

*Most of us are so caught up in **doing** and **having** that we have missed the point of being human. We have forgotten how to **be**.*

meeting, or the big stuff like divorce, redundancy, bankruptcy and debilitating illness, we have a choice in how we respond. It's well-documented that people who meditate regularly have a greatly reduced stress response. Not only are their physiological stress-indicators lower than average but they also report an inner sense of calm, are less likely to develop stress-related illness and show reversed signs of ageing. The difference between meditators and non-meditators is that the former do not get lost in thinking. They have learnt to simply relax and let go of the storylines. And in deep relaxation, you see Life *as it is* ... not how you feel about it!

The Gift of the Moment

There's a myth perpetuated in spiritual circles that we should get rid of the mind. There's an idea that enlightenment – the pinnacle of spiritual achievement – means that we live in a bubble of bliss completely untouched by thinking or feeling. But this is far from the truth!

Traditional disciplines often beat the mind into submission with sophisticated techniques such as mantra repetition, prayers and complex visualizations. And New Age methods aim for transcendence of the mind by focusing on angelic realms, ascended masters and other such higher states of consciousness. I've found that meeting the mind with such a violent or derogatory attitude just doesn't work! A newcomer to meditation practice recently explained how she was not able to shut out her thoughts. She complained that the more she tried to keep them out, the more insistent they became until she felt more stressed at the end of her meditation than before.

I explained that we cannot free ourselves from the tyranny of mind by using force or trickery, for what we resist always persists! In fact, mind itself is not the problem.

But our identification with it is. In other words, ego has identified with the contents of mind believing them to be real and therefore giving them the power to create our reality. Whatever we invest our belief in grows in strength. So, if we use the mind to fight or control the mind, we end up strengthening our ego. We might feel better because it's a spiritual ego but true freedom continues to elude us.

Instead of pushing against it, we move beyond mind by entering more deeply into it with the light of our presence. In other words, we become more present with whatever is arising without having to change it: we simply rest in the truth of *what is*. If you bring your absolute presence to each thought as it arises, it will lose its urgency. Yes, it's inevitably followed by another thought and yet another, ad infinitum. But when you bring your full attention to what is happening right here in *this* moment, a strange phenomenon happens: the thought dissolves! And if you keep staying present as each thought arises – and the next and the next – all thinking evaporates!

Thinking about the past and the future means you operate in the horizontal dimension. In the horizontal, there is always a "moving towards" or a "moving away from" but

*The thing is, the past died a long time ago and the future is yet to be born, so neither of them actually exist: time is an illusion. The only reality there is, exists in **this** very moment.*

never a simple resting in the OKness of *what is*. It is this restlessness of the mind that gives rise to fear and keeps us victims of life's shifting circumstances.

Whenever I find myself getting scared I know I'm not being present and I have to reign myself in and ask myself: "What is true here?" The thing is, the past died a long time ago and the future is yet to be born, so neither of them actually exist: time is an illusion. The only reality there is, exists in *this* very moment. The whole of Life is a seamless series of present moments. When I remember that only *now* exists and I truly allow myself to experience it as a reality, then I am immediately liberated from the tyranny of my mind.

When you relinquish the need to control Life, you find yourself falling into the gap between thoughts. And in this gap, you discover the gift of the moment. It's a timeless freedom that is untarnished by what *did* happen and what *might* happen.

The Art of Meditation

I used to go to a yoga class where the teacher always punctuated the postures with a firm "Meditate, concentrate!" I wanted to jump up and tell her meditation is not concentration! It is not a *doing*, rather it is a state of *being*.

Meditation is a deep relaxation into the simplicity of silent awareness. This means you become a witness. There's such a tendency to label and judge every experience we have. We're constantly comparing, always making something or someone better or worse than something or someone else. I like the phrase I once heard a spiritual teacher use: "Mind is always putting up or putting down." When we "put up" we feel inferior and when we "put down" we feel superior. It's one of ego's favorite games!

When you walk past the beggar on the street, do you respond with either disgust or pity? Either way, you have judged his situation as worse than yours: you have "put down." When you see that famous movie-star on TV, do you respond with either adulation or envy? Either way, you have judged her situation as better than yours: you have "put up." There's nothing wrong with compassion or appreciation but there's a world of difference between comparison and clear-seeing. The former is a function of ego and creates separation. The latter arises from the clarity of an open heart and creates oneness.

You cannot stop thoughts any less than you can stop waves on the ocean. But you can stop judging, labeling and comparing. I invite you to look around right now, wherever you are. Do you see "Rain again; goddamn weather!?" Or do you simply see drops of wet falling in patterns on the dazzling earth? Do you see "Sun is out, life is good!?" Or do you simply see bright light warming skin? Dropping the habit of labeling, judging and comparing is a great way to practice equanimity or "seeing all things as equal." Things are not intrinsically good or bad, they simply are as they are. You can even stop naming altogether! Imagine looking at a flower. Do you see "red rose?" Or can you simply rest in that wordless place beyond form? Instead of *thinking* about the flower, try just *being* with it and allowing its essence to merge with yours. You'll find that as all notions of "red rose" fall away, you are left basking in the simplicity of silent awareness.

You can also practice equanimity towards yourself. As you go about your day, notice how when you have limiting thoughts – such as "I'm not sure I'll ever succeed," or "I can't afford that," or "Life's just too difficult!" – you berate yourself for not being perfect, powerful or spiritual enough. And when you have expansive thoughts – such as "I feel on top of the world," or "I am truly abundant," or "Life's a magical playground" – you congratulate yourself for being so perfect, powerful or spiritual.

But what if these thoughts were no more solid than clouds in the sky? What if the only weight they bore was the importance you assign to them? When you stop being entranced by your own thoughts, they lose their power. When you neither resist them nor chase them but instead

Meditation is a deep relaxation into the simplicity of silent awareness.

relax into unbounded acceptance, you will see that they are not the truth. How can the truth be contained by thinking when thinking is just one small part of who you are?

When you open wide to welcome everything – without judging, comparing, labeling or even naming – the gossamer-thin veil of mind dissolves to reveal the naked brilliance of that within which mind appears. It's called the silence of Being. Silence is always accessible to you, right here in *this* moment. This is the art of meditation. It's not something you do for twenty minutes a day and then fall back into unconsciousness. You cannot wait for some later date or time to become aware: you can only be aware in *this* moment. And neither do you have to become a Buddhist: you are Buddha-nature *now*.

Of course, it does help to put some time aside each day for developing silent awareness. We've spent so much of our lives lost in the hubbub of thinking that we need to become

*Silence is always accessible to you, right here in **this** moment. This is the art of meditation.*

still enough to hear the silence of our true nature. I know from experience that it takes practice to develop equanimity. Having a set daily time in which to do this is like exercising an underused muscle. But it takes more than just a few minutes a day. Ultimately, meditation is a way of life.

Whatever you are doing, you can choose to get carried away by your storylines, or you can let them all float by whilst you remain anchored in the spaciousness of *this* moment. All activity takes place within the truth of silence. It's just a matter of changing the focus of your attention.

Silence is the nature of Existence: it underpins everything that happens. By mastering the art of meditation in *every* moment, you align yourself with cosmic order and life becomes unencumbered by ego's need for control. By attuning to the essential truth of silence, you discover the truth of who you are.

In silence, the *you* that you *think* you are disappears. And the glory of who you *really* are is revealed.

Sky Mind

It is said that we only use ten percent of our mind's full capacity. Whilst this so-called "fact" is hard to prove, there certainly seems to be a vast reservoir of creative intelligence we have not yet tapped into. Except perhaps by those few individuals throughout history who have achieved full enlightenment of Christ-consciousness. What if we too could harness this power? My feeling is that if we could, we would know the mind of God!

It seems to me that the ten percent of mind we habitually use is the domain of ego whereas the other 90 percent is the kingdom of Heaven. The former is shackled by its identification with linear thought. The latter is as free and limitless as the open sky. Just as clouds drift by and yet the sky remains unchanged, so do our thoughts come and go and yet who we are remains. We are vaster than we imagine, far more powerful than we dare. We tend to play it small, believing what we have been taught about three-dimensional reality. But beyond the material realm is a world so dazzlingly beautiful it would blow our small minds. Beyond that which appears and disappears is the infinite intelligence that orchestrated the whole show!

Nothing is separate from this divine power. It just seems to be that way when looked at through the myopic lens of small mind. And that includes us. We are so much more than just a head on legs! No wonder scientists can't prove that we only use ten percent of our minds: they've been looking in the wrong place! Thinking mind may be located in the brain but we enter the kingdom of Heaven through our hearts.

Perhaps the 90 percent of mind that science cannot find is not confined to a space-time location. Perhaps it is just like the sky, everywhere and nowhere all at once. Sky Mind is the vertical dimension of infinite potential, the space within which miracles happen. Miracles come not only in the form of turning water into wine, but also as the little nudges that awaken us to the blessedness of Life. They come in the form of insights, inspirations and synchronicities. Like when we suddenly see the bigger picture and realize that everything that has ever happened to us has been exactly what we needed for our growth ... and we feel gratitude. And like when we experience an unexpected breakthrough and some aspect of our old belief system falls away ... leaving us with the thrill of liberation. Or like when the stranger we bump into at a time of confusion or crisis turns out to be an angel who lifts us into a new phase of our life … and we are forever transformed.

And what is a miracle if not a shift in perception? When we choose to see with the unbounded eyes of love instead of with the tight-fistedness of fear, we stop trying to figure it all out with our heads and allow Source to take care of it all. In our minds, life is a problem to be solved. In God's mind, everything is a part of the divine plan. We have the choice to step outside of the illusion of our horizontal reality and awaken to the perfection of God's world. All we have to do is open our hearts.

A friend of mine recently emailed me a wonderful true story that demonstrates the power of love to create miracles. A boy born 43 years ago in the USA was brain-damaged at birth and unable to control his limbs. Doctors advised his parents to put him into an institution as he was classified

Sky Mind is the vertical dimension of infinite potential, the space within which miracles happen.

as brain-dead. But the father had faith that his son was more than a vegetable and wouldn't do it. Instead, the boy was eventually rigged up with a computer so he could communicate and as it turned out he was highly intelligent. At the age of 11 he asked his father to take him on a five-mile charity run. Despite a total lack of fitness, the father ran with his son in a wheelchair and the boy communicated that it was the first time in his life that he didn't feel disabled.

That day changed both their lives. From being unable to run more than a mile and never having learnt to swim, the father now pushes, pulls and carries his son with him in marathons and triathlons, competing with young able-bodied men at national and international levels and earning him the title of The Strongest Dad in the World. The father is now 65 and the son is 43 and they still do it: just to "see the smile" on the son's face. And as if that's not remarkable enough, two years ago, the father suffered a mild heart attack and doctors told him that had he not been in such fantastic shape he would have died 15 years ago. So, you see, they saved each other's lives!

I watched a video clip of the two men at different stages of their lives together and I was amazed at the radiance that surrounds them both. This so easily could have been a story of abject misery, proof that Our Father really is cruel and unjust. But instead, it is a story of a life blessed by grace.

Amazing Grace

When I was a child, I believed there was an invisible higher power that knew how all the details of Life were interwoven even though, to me, events appeared to be random. In other words, I had faith. It kept me going when things got tough and it filled me with a sense of grace when things seemed to amazingly fall into place.

As I grew older, however, I lost this faith and life became meaningless. With perfect symmetry – although I couldn't see it at the time – as I stopped trusting Existence to support me, so did circumstances appear to become increasingly difficult. It was a downward spiral into depression. But it was only when life really hit rock bottom that I realized I had a choice: I could continue to see all the things that were wrong and complain about my fate or I could start taking notice of what I might be grateful for. Since I'd tried the former and it brought me no happiness, I decided to try the latter.

By being grateful for the everyday things the big things miraculously began to change and new opportunities presented themselves to me. With time, I saw once more that a benevolent force was operating behind the scenes and I was filled with a sense of being blessed. I realized that gratitude – just like happiness – is a conscious choice we have to make. It's not that we wait for good things to happen and then we are grateful: it doesn't work that way! Rather, it's that we choose to be grateful for what we do have and then good things happen.

Even when we are at our lowest point, we can find something to be grateful for. We can dig deep and find gratitude for the simple things, for the things we take for granted, for the miracle of Life itself. Gratitude is a choice granted to us in *every* moment. And when we choose it, something amazing happens: Life is filled with grace.

Whenever someone asks me what grace means I must admit I still stumble for words. For it is an inexplicable sense of perfection or flow that cannot be grasped by the mind, only experienced in the deepest part of our beings. It's what happens when we make ourselves available to the infinite love that surrounds us at all times. Except that we are usually too busy feeling sorry for ourselves to notice it. Even when things are terrible, when the worst thing we could imagine has happened, we can choose to open to the deeper meaning and see the perfection in the bigger picture. Sometimes we need to be struck by a thunderbolt in order to wake up from the bondage of limited thinking. Everything that happens is designed for our spiritual growth: there are no accidents or mistakes in the divine plan. It's what Ram Dass calls "fierce grace."

When we choose to see *everything* as a gift from God, grace arrives as a blessing to open our eyes to the awesome beauty of life. My feeling is that grace is becoming more available to us these days. Perhaps this is a strange thing to say considering we live at a time when our very existence is threatened by global events. But even in the midst of such a precarious situation, there is a new vibration emerging that promises to make our wildest dreams come true. I see it when I look around at the increasing numbers of people from all walks of life who are shedding old belief systems and awakening to a new paradigm based on Love and Truth. Very often, this comes through in the form of a book or a

It's not that we wait for good things to happen and then we are grateful: it doesn't work that way! Rather, it's that we choose to be grateful for what we do have and then good things happen.

film that finds its way into mainstream culture and stretches the boundaries of what we call reality. And I hear it when I am told transformational stories by people I'd never imagine would make the leap. And I feel it every time I am touched by the invisible hands of angels guiding me on my path in life.

It's as if the veils between worlds are a little thinner than they used to be and all we need to do is reach out and ask that we be shown the light. These are amazing times that we live in, when the possibility of transformation is closer than it ever has been before. All we have to do is have faith.

Entering the Gateway of Mind

There's a simple meditation you can do at any time, wherever you are and whatever you are doing. In essence, it just brings you into the present moment and frees you from the tyranny of thinking. Perhaps you'd like to try it now? After all there's no time like the present!

OK, just relax your awareness so that it softens around the edges. No straining to push anything away, no contraction in the mind. Most likely you will become acutely aware of your thinking. Simply allow these thoughts to float by, don't chase them or try to shut them out. If your eyes are open then you will also be aware of what you see and maybe also what you hear and smell. Once again, simply allow all these sensations and thoughts to float through your awareness. Allow your awareness to expand so it is vast and limitless, open and free ... just like the sky.

Each time you find yourself fascinated by what appears on the screen of your consciousness and there is a habitual pull to follow it with your mind, just *STOP*! Take a moment to notice the tendency to get lost in thinking. And then simply relax your mind and allow everything to float through, as if your mind was permeable. You might notice how everything seems to appear out of nothingness and then disappear back into nothingness. Allow your awareness to rest more deeply in this nothingness, this empty space between thoughts. Soften the edges of your consciousness, resting in the vastness of silence that is beyond all thinking. See how thinking is just such a tiny part of it all. And how silence is infinite. Open wide to allow all thinking to pass through. See how thoughts may come and go and yet that within which thoughts appear still exists. In the eternal *now* of silent awareness, the essential nature of *this* moment remains untouched.

This open awareness – limitless and free like the sky – is available to you in *every* moment of *every* day. It doesn't matter what you are doing. What matters is that you remember that *being* is the backdrop within which all doing takes place. Whenever you catch yourself getting lost in thinking, worrying about what might or might not happen ... just *STOP!* Take a moment to refocus your attention. Tune in to the infinite silence that is here, resting deep inside *this* moment.

For *this* moment is the only one that exists. And the only one that matters.

Chapter 5
EMBRACING WHO YOU ARE:
The Gateway of Self

The drama of life unfolds from the moment we emerge from our mother's womb. So enthralling is this technicolor movie called *My Life* that we very quickly get pulled away from our original innocence. And before we know it, we are a million miles away from the perfection of our essential nature.

Far from the truth of who we really are, we search for security. And so we cling to *my* body, *my* intellect, *my* emotions. We hold tight to *my* success, *my* power, *my* happiness. Or even to *my* failure, *my* weakness, *my* unhappiness. Making something *mine* gives us a sense of being somebody. After all, if you've forgotten who you are, isn't it best to create a new definition of yourself? But in identifying with the world of inner and outer phenomena, we make a fundamental error: we allow ourselves to be defined by what we have, do, think or feel. In other words, we lose ourselves in the transient world of form.

The journey of awakening requires that we ask ourselves: "Who am I?" This one question has the power to propel us through the gateway of self and into the abyss of Being where God is waiting to catch us. And in allowing ourselves to be held by that to which we cannot cling, we remember that who we are is far more than the fleeting image of *me*. In the timeless zone of splendid stillness, we discover we are that which is never born or never dies.

And in this realization, we come home to the freedom of our true nature.

The Mask of Personality

We're all shaped by family and social conditioning. From the day we are born, the wide open space of our being twists into patterns that fit our parents' expectations. We're so sensitive to every subtle fluctuation in emotional temperature that we retract a millimeter here and tighten a centimeter there in order to protect ourselves. Over the years, fear warps our essential love-nature and the brilliant smile of our true face moulds into the mask of personality. It sounds terrible but it's an inevitable part of growing up!

The real problem comes when the ego-defenses we erect solidify into roles we are comfortable with and we end up thinking that this is who we are. Identification with the shell of protection around the core of our essence means we are limited by our own self-definitions. Identifying with "I am a successful businessman," or "I am a caring mother" – or any other description – means you do not allow yourself to grow beyond these roles. Being firmly entrenched in "I am hard-working / easy-going / nice / nasty / heterosexual / gay / English / Chinese / Catholic / Muslim," makes it harder to discover the truth of your unbounded nature.

That's not to say that we can erase our personal history. We've all got stories. These might be stories of excruciating failure or jubilant victory, stories of grief, despair, hope or magic. It's what makes us human. Everything we experience is colored by our thoughts, emotions, moods and memories and becomes a sub-plot on the stage of our lives. As sentient beings living in a three-dimensional world, this cannot be otherwise. But what *can* be different is whether we identify with these stories. In other words, whether we make them our own. In my work, I meet so many spiritual seekers who think they've awakened because they've dropped their story of "conventionality" and become "alternative". Frequently, they are healers or self-help teachers. But all they have done is substitute one story for another, perhaps more preferable, one.

Holding tight to any storyline – however spiritual, enlightened or cosmic – means you are still a victim of your biography. Far from being free, you are trapped in a prison of your own making. The only way to discover the verticality of your true nature is to ask yourself: "Who am I?" Self-inquiry loosens identification with biography and ultimately reveals the illusory nature of self.

But before you can transcend yourself, you need to make friends with yourself. Each time you inquire into who you are, you reveal another layer of yourself and have the opportunity to befriend this part. The journey of awakening

The journey of awakening requires that you dive deep inside into uncharted territory and embrace your totality.

---

requires that you dive deep inside into uncharted territory and embrace your totality. It means seeing through the false layers of protection and baring your heart to the world and to God. It means loving every part of yourself and yet knowing you are more than just these parts.

Beyond the details of your story, you are that which cannot be tainted by definitions. Behind the mask of personality, you are the purity of perfect wholeness.

Making Friends With Your Monsters

As children we love to express ourselves spontaneously. But family, friends, school and society all have their own code of conduct. Mostly it's our natural, instinctual and emotional energies that get labeled bad or wrong. I remember always being told to be good by my parents. Any display of anger or sadness was promptly squashed and so I grew up unable to express either. Unfortunately, whatever we deny has a habit of coming back to bite us and I ended up with suicidal tendencies until I learnt how to release my rage and my grief.

And it's not just the difficult energies that are feared. The natural exuberance of children is an embarrassment to many adults. Perhaps you remember being told to stop making a fool of yourself or to calm down and behave? And how many of us in our early years have been severely berated for enjoying pleasurable body sensations? Every baby is born vibrating with sexual energy and yet this is most often met with confusion and disgust.

Our dependency on our parents for physical well-being as well as for human warmth drives us to maintain this bond at all costs. If we display an emotion that causes a retraction of love or attention in our parents, we immediately label it as bad. It's accompanied by the devastating belief that we are not lovable just as we are. The unbearable shame of feeling imperfect and therefore unworthy of unconditional love means we fragment. We split off the unwanted parts of ourselves and send them into the shadowlands where we cannot see them. Over time, we forget they were ever a part of us. In other words, we sacrifice our authentic self.

But banishing energies we are not comfortable with does not actually make them go away. In fact, these unloved parts just go underground and develop a secret life of their own. You cannot destroy a natural energy, but it can destroy you. Every part of your psyche is alive and needs to breathe. When it is buried, the natural flow of its energy becomes distorted and seeks expression in surreptitious ways. Just when you thought you had it tucked away tidily, it sneaks up on you and gives you quite a surprise! An unconscious energy is like a monster: it is ugly, mean and very destructive.

One of my ex-boyfriends carried unacknowledged anger for years. To everyone else he was Mr Charming, always smiling, easy-going and fun to hang around with. But every once in a while – mostly after a drink or two when his guard was down – the seething monster of rage would erupt. As I was the person closest to him, I bore the brunt of his outbursts. He was almost always filled with remorse afterwards and blamed it on the "demon drink!"

This kind of denial of what we don't want to see in ourselves is always at the root of abuse, whether it is verbal, emotional or physical. It's always a cover-up for deep-down pain and shame. Research shows that perpetrators of violence are frequently victims of childhood violence themselves. The longer something lives in the darkness of unconsciousness, the more likely it is to burst out in destructive ways.

In having the courage to make friends with our own monsters, they are restored to their true nature. They stop being ugly demons waiting to pounce on you. Instead they become natural energies that inform you how you feel so that you can make appropriate choices in your life. Ultimately, it's a choice between love and fear. It's a choice between tightening into familiar shapes that constrict you and opening softly into what is really happening. By choosing the latter – even though it feels scary or uncomfortable – you transform your monsters into allies.

Every part of your psyche is alive and needs to breathe. When it is buried, the natural flow of its energy becomes distorted and seeks expression in surreptitious ways.

Going beyond right and wrong heals the split in your psyche and sets you on the return journey home to your true nature. And when you are totally at home with yourself, you will be at home with the world. Embracing yourself just as you are means you can embrace the world just *as it is*!

A peaceful world arises when we are all at peace with ourselves.

Reclaiming Your Authentic Self

Reclaiming your authentic self is one of the toughest journeys you can make but it's worth all the gold in the world!

The adventure of self-discovery most often begins with a sense that something is missing. We can spend our whole lives with a nagging sense of incompleteness and yet do nothing about it. Instead, we try to fill the hole with food, sex, relationships, power, money or the ultimate high. But if we're lucky, we wake up one day and realize that none of these work. When we hear the deeper call from within, the authentic search for what is true can begin. And in being willing to meet what has been denied in ourselves for so long, we invite the fullness of love to enter our lives and to make us whole once again.

As you learn to make friends with yourself, you relax beneath the hard exterior that defines you and sink into the soft center of honest vulnerability. And right here – in your heart – is an innocent child who feels everything in its delicious intensity. It is your heart that was wounded each time love was withdrawn from you but it is your ego that has numbed the pain by creating a fortress of lies.

When these old strategies have outlived their usefulness we often find that the outer structure of our lives starts to crumble. Marriage, career, finances and home frequently get fraught with difficulty, conflict and confusion when there's something urging you to grow beyond your limitations. When things start falling apart, you can be sure that the child that lives in your heart is calling you to awaken to your full potential. And until you truthfully embrace this neglected part of yourself, you remain a child in an adult's body.

Strange though it may sound, what we call normal adult behavior is very often our wounded child living itself out through us. It's worth taking a closer look at this because the more you have denied your wounded child, the more

When we hear the deeper call from within, the authentic search for what is true can begin.

power it has to distort your perception of reality. There's something called a "trigger" in psycho-babble terminology that aptly describes what happens when we're unaware of our woundedness. A trigger causes us to react unconsciously to situations that stir deep down feelings we have long ago banished. Because these feelings go hand in hand with our sense of unworthiness, our ego puts up a defense barrier to protect us from feeling the true depth of our hurt. Whilst this appears to be a useful "band aid," it has the side-effect of catapulting us into the past. It means we're not living in the full brilliance of *now*.

Triggering is a frequent cause of arguments in relationships as it's the place where we're the most vulnerable. Other common "trigger-happy" situations relate to our parents, dealing with the boss at work, negotiating finances, and moving home. The specific kind of defense we employ in any given situation is based on our conditioning and happens involuntarily. It depends on the behavioral responses we have learnt from family and society, our genetic predisposition and our karma. But every defense mechanism has the same aim: to protect us from feeling the shame of being unlovable.

Here are some common defense mechanisms that get triggered·

Guilt

Guilt is a great cover-up for real feelings. "It must be my fault" firmly puts the lid on whatever feelings we may have learned to label as unacceptable. When we deny our authentic expression, we build up a reservoir of grief, desolation and despair Guilt is a way of making sure we never get near the horror of what lurks inside. Unfortunately, it also dampens our joy and delight. It's like a heavy suit of armor that keeps you from experiencing the vibrancy of life.

Blame

This is another great deflector of real feelings. "It's your fault" slams the door shut on true communication. In the blame-game you're constantly batting the ball back at your opponent. Because both of you are so busy attacking and defending, you can avoid sharing your vulnerability. Whilst this may reduce the risk of being hurt, it also means you stay isolated from each other.

Numbing out

"I feel nothing" is a clue that you have spaced out, shut down, contracted or withdrawn. In other words, you are unavailable emotionally. In the short term, this is a very effective way of not feeling anything uncomfortable. But in the long-term, habitual numbing out leads to low level depression.

Addictions

Addictive behavior can be obvious as in drug abuse, alcoholism or eating disorders, but it can also be very subtle and we all do it to some degree or another. It requires ruthless honesty and true presence to be able to detect it. Basically, if you habitually smoke, drink, take recreational drugs, eat, shop or have sex *in order to feel better*, then you're either stuffing down your feelings or you're filling up the hole left behind by numbing out.

Co-dependency

If your self-worth depends on another person's love or approval, then you don't know who you really are or what you feel. If you try to please, cajole or seduce in order to be loved, then you will be unable to reveal the totality of your authentic self and true intimacy cannot bloom.

Control

If you really need things to turn out the way you want them to in order to feel OK, if you are time-obsessed, if you are a workaholic or if you have rigid routines and fixed opinions about what you can and can't do, then the bottom line is that you don't trust life to carry you safely. In controlling your environment, you are attempting to keep at bay your own feelings of discomfort and fear when life shows signs of being unpredictable. It's a losing battle because the nature of life is change.

Compliancy

If you find it difficult to assert yourself or it's impossible for you to say no, if you are a "people pleaser" or always try to do "the right thing," then you are unable to reveal your authentic self for fear of being rejected. Rebelliousness is the flip side of compliancy: by going against others or the world in an aggressive way, you make sure you are not rejected first.

I'm familiar with all of the above as I've tried out every one of them at some point of my life. Until I found out that they just weren't going to bring me the pain-free life I was hoping for! When the veil lifted from my eyes and I saw that all my attempts to get love from my relationships, my friends, my work, my life and from God were futile, I realized that I was simply avoiding the pain inside. And what really hurt was that I was stuck in a world that revolved around me, unable to offer anything because I was empty inside.

One of the most important spiritual lessons I received was an answer to my question: "What will I receive if I risk opening myself up to loving Life *as it is*?" The answer that came back was: "There are no Brownie points in Heaven." I translated this to mean that there is no guarantee of a reward to make you feel better, because love is not self-centered. I had been withholding my love from the world because I wanted to make sure that if I risked opening my heart I would be rewarded with ever-lasting happiness. I

was still operating from a personal perspective, seeking
to stay safe. Contemplating the answer to my question
led me to see that love requires a sacrifice of small self. It
requires a letting go into the void of selflessness without any
expectation of outcome.

In a horizontal reality, we fear that we won't get what
we think we need in order to feel whole. And so we shrink
back from freely giving our gifts to the world. When we wake
up to the goodness of our essential nature, we become God-
centered. When we open fully to each moment as it happens,
we become one with the flow of Existence. And in this vertical
reality, giving and receiving are meaningless because love is
that which cannot be grasped.

In the openness of Being, love is the endless flow of an
unobstructed heart.

From Wound to Wonderment

The heart is a conduit for the river of Life. An open heart
responds to circumstances with moment-to-moment feeling.
Tightening into defensive patterns constricts the natural

flow so that the heart loses its ability to feel. Instead, there's such a build-up of blocked energy that there's an explosion of emotion.

Emotion is self-justified rage in which you're absolutely sure that it was his (or her) fault. Or swamping sadness in which you just can't bear to go on any more. Or maybe paralyzing fear in which you are scared stiff of what might happen. It's always a reaction based on the past. Unlike emotion, feeling has no storyline attached to it. It's a simple response to *this* moment. Feelings are always the truth of *what is*, whereas emotion is a lie created out of what *was*.

When feelings have been denied over and over again, we forget the wholeness of our essential nature. The deepest wound we carry in our heart is the pain of this forgetting. But when the pain gets too much to bear, the only way out is to dive in. Breathing into the jagged edge of resistance reveals the truth of your broken heart. And in releasing a lifetime's unshed tears for the authentic you that got lost amidst all the shoulds and shouldn'ts, the river of grief heals your wounds. It's not just the big traumas that need to be grieved for, but also the day-to-day hurts: the broken dreams and loss of faith, the failures, mistakes and disappointments.

It's worth remembering that even the tiniest hurt ignored creates a fracture that hardens into closure. The "biggies" – such as physical and emotional abuse, childhood neglect, or loss of a loved one – are wounds that need to be cradled in the tenderest part of your heart and require extreme sensitivity and loving patience. Sometimes this requires the help of a skilled specialist, such as a therapist or healer. But it is to the everyday situations that we can really turn our attention to welcome in the miracle of healing.

Every interaction we have with another human being – whether it be the postman or our long-term partner – and every transaction we make in the world – whether it be shopping for groceries or negotiating a business deal – and every project we undertake – whether it be baking a cake or climbing the highest mountain – carries with it the possibility of suffering when things don't turn out how we'd like them. But each of these also provides us with the

---

Feelings are always the truth of **what is**, *whereas emotion is a lie created out of what* **was***.*

opportunity to choose the healing power of love.

Whether we seek expert assistance or not, in the end it is our own willingness to soften where it hurts that matters. The gentle meeting of pain in the bowl of awareness calls in loving kindness where it had once been forgotten. Conscious surrender to this vigilant openness initiates a deep cleansing that takes you from anger to sadness to betrayal to shame to loneliness and every emotional hue and tone in between. It's an on-going practice that unravels layers of pain and takes you through the rawness of emotion to the delicacy of feeling. It's not something that we *do*, but something that happens when we are truly willing to meet each moment *as it is*. It's the honest inquiry into *this* moment that sets you on the journey from fragmentation to wholeness.

I am often asked why the path of awakening has to be, at times, so difficult. Isn't there a way of enjoying the benefits of a spiritual life without having to go through the pain? Well, the exquisite texture of a truly spiritual life comes from having had the courage to stay open in the midst of heart-wrenching agony. When you can open your heart even in hell, then the kingdom of Heaven is yours. I know this from my own experience and I have seen it time and again in other people whose lives have been transformed by allowing themselves to feel honestly and completely into each moment as it arises.

Sometimes we mistake victimhood for grief. But getting stuck in Poor Me is not the same as plumbing the depths of your anguish. Over-identification with wounding is a common trap that creates a self-perpetuating lie. Honest grief means going beyond your storylines, however justified they may appear to be. It means diving into the totality of your wounding and opening your arms to welcome the good, the bad and the ugly. And when you keep opening to meet whatever appears without stopping long enough to create a story about it, you eventually drop into the place where there is no story. In loving your wounded child without limits, it can finally release its gift of love to you.

I am reminded of the story of Ananda who was a disciple of Buddha. He had been at his master's side for 42 years and when Buddha died, Ananda remained by his side weeping. The other disciples chastised him for his ignorance: "Buddha died absolutely fulfilled. You should be rejoicing." Ananda replied: "You do not understand. I am not weeping for him, but for myself. After all these years so close to him, I have not awakened and now it is too late." And so Ananda stayed awake all night meditating deeply on his grief. By the morning, he was enlightened.

What this story tells us is that when we are willing to meet our pain in the fullness of awareness, there is a possibility for transformation. Deep acceptance of the ache in our hearts transforms our woundedness to wonderment. Wonderment means we live in the wonder of *now*. It is a reclamation of our divinity in which our wounded child is reborn as the Golden Child. The divine spark at our core lives in the purity of presence and in the playfulness of delight. Every moment is an adventure to be met with eyes wide open and belly soft, even when things get tough.

When life is no longer contaminated by the baggage of your past, the mystery of Life unfolds and your soul's unique purpose is revealed. From an expanded perspective, you get to see how every part of your life – however painful – is *exactly* what you need for your evolution. And in this revelation, there's a deep relaxation. There's an unquestionable trust in the divine blueprint of your life.

The truth is God never abandoned you. In every moment, He has been at your side ... nudging you to take the final leap into freedom.

The Jump to No-Self

The jump to no self is the final frontier. Once you walk through the doorway of your heart, you are faced with probably the most difficult choice you can make. As you stand at the edge of your being, you are asked to let go of the very thing that defines *you* as you: your sense of self.

Self-ownership is the last obstacle to true liberation. Once you have reclaimed your authentic self it is tempting to bask in a kind of comfort zone. But once wholeness is restored, growth does not stop here. As the stagnancy of spiritual smugness sets in, you inevitably sense that the journey is incomplete.

Self-ownership is the pervasive sense of *me* as a separate entity. It is the sense of *my* body, *my* thoughts and *my* emotions. It is *my* life existing in a bubble with *me* at the center whilst everything else exists outside this bubble. If what goes on outside of me has a positive impact on *my* life then I feel *good*. But if it has a negative impact then I feel *bad*. It's a horizontal perspective in which I try to get the most out of life, whether it be material or spiritual. Even the search for enlightenment is based on a sense of self. From the vantage point of *me*, everything is seen in terms of loss or gain. You lose wealth, you gain power, you lose faith, you gain happiness, and so on. Eventually, you lose your life. Or so it seems.

Look deep inside and you will see that every thought arises out of nothing and returns to nothing. So how can you own it? Every feeling and every emotion arises out of nothing and returns to nothing. Every breath comes and goes. Even your body is born out of the miracle of Life and returns at death to the great mystery that is beyond Life. Thoughts, feelings, arms, legs, blood, breath arise *in* you but they are not yours. Making any of these *mine* keeps you locked in the spell of separation.

If you look deeply, you will see that there is a part of you that simply observes events, thoughts and feelings. This is the *witness*. But even the "I" that is the witness is not yours. As soon as you identify with the witness, you create a subtle separation between you and what you are witnessing. Ultimately, there is only *witnessing* itself. This is the

---

Self-ownership is the last obstacle to true liberation.

pristine awareness within which everything appears. You cannot claim this for it does not belong to you. That within which you appear exists anyway, whether *you* do or not. It is the ground of Being from which we are born and into which we die. Every single thing that appears in Existence is just a ripple on the surface of the ocean of consciousness. All forms are impermanent manifestations that arise out of eternal formlessness. And this includes *you* and your life. You cannot own your life, for you *are* Life!

The jump to no-self is a dive into the verticality of Being in which all ownership evaporates. The profound realization that you are not in charge of your life but rather Life is that which simply expresses itself through you, allows you to relax deeply into whatever is happening now. The truth is *this is all there is*. And you are not separate from this. This is both a deeply humbling and a hugely empowering place to come to because ultimately, *God is all there is* and you are not separate from God.

Letting go into no-self is a conscious surrender of your life to God. It's a moment-to-moment choosing of the grandeur of love over the small-minded concerns of ego. When you are receptive to the higher calling that emanates from an inner stillness, your will becomes aligned with Divine Will. And your life becomes an expression of the divinity of your true nature.

The Flower of Compassion

When you have the courage to lose your self, you gain the world. Instead of small me getting lost inside the Big World, the vastness of the world is contained within you.

When you no longer need to protect yourself from Life nor try to get something from it, you stop being selfish and become selfless. Of course, you don't just become a martyr sacrificing your own well-being for others. You still have a body that needs taking care of, you still have feelings, you still have a home, finances and family to take care of. But you do not own these things and you are not identified with them.

Selflessness means that all these things have been given to you by Existence so that you may take care of them. Your life becomes an act of service. It's a gift to the world simply because it is flowing through you. You stop trying to get love or even to be more loving, for now you simply are Love. In selflessness, every act – however minuscule or grandiose – is an expression of love that bubbles up from the deep well at your core. Even when things appear to go wrong, even when you appear to have made a mistake or to have failed, if it has arisen from a place of non-ownership then it is Love in Action.

Love is simply the radiant openness of Being. Living in the radiance of love means you have compassion for your own suffering and for the suffering of the world. It means your heart is open to the violence, injustice, greed and ignorance you see around the globe, in your next-door neighbor and in your self. It doesn't necessarily mean you have to fix anything or even be nice. What it means is that you can *be* with the suffering without either reacting in anger or collapsing into hopelessness. There's evidence from research into trauma that simply listening to someone's story of suffering has a more healing effect than offering solutions to the problem.

Compassion means you recognize that whatever harm is done to any other living being – whether it be human, animal, plant or planet – is also harm done to you, because we are all interconnected. It also means you have compassion for those who do harm, because violence is suffering that arises from a deep sense of alienation from life. Even those who do harm to others are a part of us. In the vertical dimension of Being, there is no separation: we are all manifestations of God, it's just that some of us have forgotten this. It is from this deep understanding that *we are all one* that *right action* can arise naturally. Compassion is not something you *do* because you think it is a good thing, but something that flowers when you have let go of who you are not.

A compassionate world is one in which everything we do, say, think or touch is filled with the fragrance of our deepest truth. It is only when we take full responsibility for our journey into spiritual maturity that the world will grow beyond immature self-centeredness. When we reclaim our inherent divinity, the world will be reborn as a place filled with joy and wonder. But it is up to each and every one of us to ask ourselves if we are prepared to risk losing everything in order to gain the world.

Are you truly prepared to take the leap into the liberation of Being? Are you willing to let go into the groundlessness of your Sky-nature?

Entering the Gateway of Self

You might like to try this beautiful meditation. Over the years, I have used it numerous times and especially when I have felt very small and scared. You can do it anytime and anywhere. With practice, you can even do it whilst you are talking to someone or involved in some task. It's a great way to remember who you are and is both healing and liberating!

Close your eyes and take a few deep conscious breaths. Now gently bring your attention to where your body might be tense and breathe into this space. On the in-breath, allow the spaciousness of unconditional love. On the out-breath, let go of any tightness or fear. Keep doing this until you feel your whole body bathed in the softness of acceptance. You may come up against some uncomfortable feelings or some negative thoughts about yourself. Simply see these for what they are ... waves in the sea of consciousness. They are not who you really are, for they come and go. Can you simply let them be? Can you keep on breathing in the love?

Let yourself dive beneath the surface of the ocean to that tender place at the center of your chest. Stay here for a few moments and give your heart some room to breathe. Soften into the hard edges, meet your resistance with acceptance. Simply stay softly open with the doubt, the fear, the anger, the ache. No judgments, no turning away. Everything is welcome here. Your heart is a safe haven for all that has been unloved, all that has been wounded. Make a home for your wounded child ... right here in your heart. Allow all the pain and all the shame to be held with love ... right here in your heart. If you like, you can imagine cradling your wounded child with the utmost tenderness ... right here in your heart. Give him or her *all* the love you never received but craved for. Envelop this child in a blanket of golden light.

Now go a little deeper. Allow your heart to break open with longing, with the piercing arrow of remembrance that takes you to your core. You are the divine spark at the center. Let your heart burst open and shower you in love, bathing in golden light. Open so wide that you disappear in the vastness of *this* moment. Free-fall into the unboundedness of your true nature, as limitless as the wide-open sky, no beginning and no ending ... just the utter simplicity of this!

And in the emptiness of Sky-nature, allow *everything* to be held ... the whole of Existence, both formless and form.

Allow everything to arise in the groundlessness of Being ... all thoughts, all emotions, all physical sensations, all ideas of who you are, all ideas of how the world is. Allow your being to contain the universe. Every single thing that exists can be held in the wide-open spaciousness of your heart. Breathe in and allow everything to rest in the compassion of your heart. Breathe out and relax deeply, resting in compassion for yourself.

Rest softly here for as long as you like, bathing in the radiance of your true nature. When you are ready, bring your attention back to your breath rising and falling in the center of your chest and to the contours of your body. And now open your eyes.

"May you be free of suffering, may you be at peace. May all beings be free of suffering, may all beings be at peace."

Chapter 6

BEHOLDING THE BELOVED:
The Gateway of Relationship

The gateway to God towers before us in jewel-encrusted glory when it comes to relationships. Except mostly we are blinded by its luminosity and end up forgetting to knock on the door!

Relationship holds the most potent possibility for liberation ... if only we could see it. It is such a powerful vehicle for awakening that the lessons come thick and fast. When we get the message and open to fully receive all that relationship has to offer, our being sings for joy and we enter the kingdom of Heaven. But in tightening around how we think relationship should be, we miss the gift and tumble into Hell.

All of our dreams and all of our nightmares live inside relationship. It is here that we experience the most pleasure, and the most pain. As any one of us can probably testify! Certainly, all of my relationships have taken me to both the giddy heights of delight and the darkest depths of despair. I always knew that relationship held the key to something special but I was looking in the wrong place. It is only when I stopped trying to get love from another person and instead had the courage to dive deep into my own heart that things started to change. When I finally saw that romantic love was a myth, the true gift of relationship revealed itself to me and transformed me in ways I could not have imagined.

Relationship has the power to awaken us to our true nature. Through deep communion with another we become the divine perfection of our essential self.

To this day, it continues to shower its blessings onto my life.

Relationship has the power to awaken us to our true nature. Through deep communion with another we become the divine perfection of our essential self. But before we can walk through the gateway and into the arms of God we need to demolish a few myths that stand in our way.

The Myth of Romantic Love

The allure of romantic love casts its spell far and wide. There probably aren't many of us who, in the most secret recesses of our hearts, don't yearn to be swept off our feet by the perfect lover. Or at least to have all our cares soothed away by marital bliss.

Unfortunately, the illusion of Happy Ever After is one that causes perhaps the most personal suffering. It's a hard one to break because the intensity of falling in love offers the possibility of the dream really coming true. The infatuation that consumes us in the early stages of a relationship is so overwhelming that we literally lose ourselves. This surrender is so deeply satisfying that for a while the world looks rosy and we float on a cloud of happiness. But let's be honest, how long does this feeling last?

Inevitably, the intoxication of passion's perfume wears off and you come back down to earth with a bump. Disillusionment sets in as conflict, pain, boredom and stagnation replace the spark of magic that brought you together in the first place. And as time goes on, that tender ache in your heart returns. It seems that love – at least *romantic* love – is not enough to keep a relationship alive.

In previous generations, the institution of marriage provided enough status, security and comfort to glue a relationship together for a lifetime even after the romantic dream had faded away. I've seen it in my parents' generation who stick by each other come hell or high water. And I've seen it in cultures where stereotypical male-female roles are still in place. In today's world, however, most of us demand something more from our relationships. No longer does a

Unfortunately, the illusion of Happy Ever After is one that causes perhaps the most personal suffering.

man need to be the breadwinner nor does a woman need to be the housewife. Education, career and earning power have freed us from the ties of convention and we are now free to experiment with new ways of relating.

And yet the myth of The Perfect Relationship stills holds us in its grip. What's more, these days we want our partner to not only adore us but also to be our playmate, our best friend, our therapist ... and, of course, to be sexy, rich and successful! Our expectations are so high that it's no wonder the dream gets shattered! But even though we may know this, we are heartbroken when it doesn't work out.

As chemistry fades and personalities clash, each unresolved conflict creates another rift and the heart hardens to protect itself from further pain. We can use our hardness to go into battle over and over again. Or we can keep the peace by compromising our values and our real feelings. Either way, it doesn't work! I know because I've tried both!

One of the most important things I have learnt about relationship is that each time we let ourselves down by hiding our truth and each time our partner lets us down because they don't live up to how we think they *should* be, love dies.

Dreams, expectations and lies are killers! Eventually, we sacrifice our authenticity for security and comfort. Or else we wait until someone else comes along who reignites the fire and off we go to repeat another variation of the same theme.

It's time we woke up and realized the true purpose of relationship.

The Power of Conscious Relationship

Because I went through so much difficulty and pain in my relationships, I finally got wise and started asking myself – and Existence – some pertinent questions. Like: "If love itself is not enough to keep a relationship alive, then what else is required?" And: "If Happy Ever After is such an illusion, then what is the secret that makes love grow?" Not to mention: "If relationship is so full of difficulty, then why bother at all?"

The answer I came up with can be summed up in one sentence: because relationship holds the greatest opportunity for transformation! Far from being a romantic illusion, love holds the key to awakening. But only if there's a willingness for personal growth. The thing I realized is that love always brings up anything that isn't love. If we could truly understand the power of this statement, we would transform our relationships and our lives forever.

Love highlights whatever hides in the darkness so that it can be made conscious. Any part of us that is tight with fear will be brought up to the surface, whether we like it or not. That's why it's so painful. The war-zone in our own psyche is reflected in the struggle with our partner.

I battled for years with my (now ex-) husband. We loved each other but we both thought it was the other's fault when things went wrong. We were so angry that the other was spoiling the love. What neither of us knew was that love was trying to heal our wounds. We were being called to go beyond old patterns that kept us enslaved to our personal history. Unfortunately, we didn't get the message.

Since then I have learnt that love is a delicate flower that needs the right environment in which to grow. And the most fertile place is in a relationship between two individuals willing to truly meet each other. Love demands that you relax the brittle defenses of false self and reveal the whole of you. The more you can embrace yourself, warts and all, the more you can embrace each other, warts and all! Spacious acceptance of yourself just as you are in *this* moment means you can meet the truth of your partner just as he or she is in *this* moment. Imagine what a relief it is when you can both relax and just be yourselves with each other!

Love is a *real* force with the power to expose old wounds and hold them up to the light until they heal. And in healing they become our gifts, our wisdom and our strength. When relationship is brought out of the dark ages into the light of conscious evolution, it becomes a potent force for personal and universal transformation. When love grows between two people it reverberates through every cell of their beings and radiates to touch others and the world around them.

If we can make our relationship conscious then we make the world conscious!

Polishing the Mirror

Relationship is such a potent force for awakening that it is like a mirror that reflects back to us all that is hidden.

Love always seeks symmetry, so whatever you disown in yourself gets projected out onto your partner and then gets reflected back to you. The equation is simple: whatever you react strongly to in your partner is what you have denied in yourself. This can be either something you absolutely detest or something you absolutely idolize.

I used to hate one of my boyfriends for being so carefree. He was always going wild at parties and stepping over social boundaries. It was a frequent cause of argument. Had I known better, I would have seen that his irresponsibility was a reflection of my tightness around proper behavior. It was I who needed to learn to let my hair down! On the other hand, I was in awe of the way he charmed people with his wit and entertaining stories and it made me feel inadequate about my quiet shyness. Over the years, I learnt that allowing the warmth of words to come alive was a hidden quality of my own.

Understanding this dynamic of "projections" is the key that transforms an entangled relationship to an enlightened one. It is so fundamental that ignoring it is like a death-sentence to relationship. Polarizing into "I'm right, you're wrong" is a clue that you have forgotten to look in the mirror.

When you can go beyond the tightness of blame and instead allow the openness of love to guide you, then relationship becomes your teacher. Transformation happens when you stop looking for how to fix what you think is wrong and start seeing what you might learn. Seeing our hidden self in the other is the gift of relationship because it takes us on a journey to wholeness.

Every time you see yourself reflected in the other, you polish the mirror of your consciousness. Polishing the mirror means the defenses that usually cloud the clarity of Sky Mind dissolve to reveal the dazzling beauty of who you really are. Behind the façade of personality is the radiance of your true nature and each time you polish the mirror it shines more brightly. Eventually, you get to see God smiling right back at you!

Navigating Deep Waters

When Kavi and I first got together we were clear we didn't want to play the same old relationship games. Both of us had been burnt badly by our previous experiences and this time

Seeing our hidden self in the other is the gift of relationship because it takes us on a journey to wholeness.

we wanted to do it consciously! Because each relationship is unique, we knew we were about to navigate uncharted terrain. We had an intuition that relationship was a doorway to the divine but we also knew that we would have to dive deep in order to find the key.

Very early on we identified two principles we would have to live by if our relationship was to live up to its promise. The first was Truth. This meant having clarity or knowing the purpose of our relationship. The questions we asked ourselves were: "Are we just stumbling through relationship, hoping that things are OK? Or is our intention to deepen into love even though we don't necessarily know how?" The second principle was Love. This meant having an open heart and allowing all possibilities. We asked ourselves: "Do we have a list of rules and expectations for how a relationship should be? Or are we willing to explore how it is and where it might take us?"

We rapidly worked out that Love and Truth were universal principles at the heart of every relationship but that they get distorted over time. In our explorations, we discovered *four* guidelines that could act as life-rafts to hold onto when the sea gets stormy and we lose sight of where we are going. These guidelines form the cornerstones of conscious relationship and apply to everyone:

Honesty

Communication of the truth is the life-blood of relationship. The number of lies we tell is equal to the distance we create between ourselves and another. We may lie about what we *do* or what we *think* but the most important lie is about how we *feel*. Very often, we may say one thing with our words and another with our behavior or our energy. For instance, we may say nice things to placate when our body is tightening into "I hate you!" Ninety-nine percent of the time we respond habitually to situations that trigger the protective mechanisms we learnt in childhood.

In order for the truth to reveal itself we need to stop and listen. It requires us to create space for open-ended exploration. It is not *what* is said that is important but the spirit of inquiry. Even "I feel nothing" can be used as a springboard to dive deeper. Only by two people being truly themselves can there be true relating. All else is a lie.

Courage

Telling the truth can be scary. How much easier it is to retract from revealing ourselves in order to keep things nice! Hearing the truth can also be scary. How much easier it is to shy away from really listening to another so that we don't have to feel discomfort!

It takes courage to tell the truth and to hear the truth. And it takes courage to even admit we're scared, to dive beneath the surface of "Oh, everything's just fine," to "Let's explore what's really going on." Having the courage to stay open is the mark of a Warrior of the Heart. A Warrior of the Heart practices swimming in deep waters just as a martial artist practices moving with the flow. Eventually, fear stops being the enemy and becomes your ally.

Responsibility

Being responsible means owning your feelings 100 percent! When you blame your partner for how you feel, you get caught up in a power battle and you lose touch with what is really going on for you. Even five percent blame means you end up in an entanglement. It doesn't matter who started it and who's right or wrong. What matters is your response to it. And this means telling the truth of how you feel and totally owning this feeling, however uncomfortable it may be. This does not mean blaming yourself either! Blaming or judging yourself means you remain a victim. And blaming or judging the other means you become the critic. These are both storylines that keep the truth hidden and create distance between you. It means you constrict the flow of love because there are two egos instead of two hearts! When each of you takes *total* responsibility for your own feelings, it makes space for the bigger picture to reveal itself. And in this space love grows.

Vulnerability

You may be a lion in the boardroom or a tiger in the bedroom but power-games do not lead to love. The sweetness of falling in love is due to a dropping of defenses that makes you vulnerable to the other. It doesn't work to ignore either big or little hurts. Nothing is too small to explore, as long as you take total responsibility for your feelings and don't blame either yourself or the other. Rather than seeing the sharing of what scares or hurts you as a sign of weakness or that there is something terribly wrong in the relationship, see it as an opportunity to create delicious intimacy.

In my relationship, whenever either of us steers away from these four life-rafts, we end up very lost. Not only do we find ourselves a million miles away from each other but we also get cut off from an essential part of ourselves. But because the rewards of getting back on track are so great – even though it might be painful or difficult – it doesn't take us long to jump back on again!

The best gift you can give not only to yourself but also to your partner is to allow relationship to be a vehicle for emotional and spiritual growth. It requires a commitment not to each other or even to the relationship itself but to the transformative nature of surrender to the *process* of relationship. To grow in consciousness together is a beautiful journey that can take you beyond a contract of limitation to an adventure of liberation.

The Alchemy of True Love

True love is limitless. It's like jumping into a vast ocean in which you cannot see the shore. When we fall in love and embark on the journey of relationship we can never be certain where it will take us. But what is certain is that holding onto a relationship too tightly squeezes out all the juice and eventually kills it!

True love requires a commitment to the internal journey and not to the external form. In being open to all possible outcomes, the shape of your relationship will form naturally. And this means being willing to let go of the relationship itself! Transformation through love can only happen when we are willing to let go of everything. And this includes our fear of being alone.

It took me a long time to learn that aloneness is not the same as loneliness. Loneliness exists in a horizontal reality. In feeling separate we look to the outside – whether to an activity, an object or a person – to make us feel connected and whole. It means we enter relationship from a place of need. Whilst need is an ingredient of relationship that should not be denied, it's also a dependency pattern that stems from childhood. If it remains unconscious, we just keep playing out unresolved issues that don't allow room for growth.

Aloneness is quite different! Aloneness exists within a vertical reality. Here, there's no separation because you are *all one*. When circumstances forced me to bring total awareness to my loneliness, I discovered the beauty and strength of aloneness. I realized that I was not dependent on another for my completeness because *I am already whole.*

There's only one way through the agony of feeling abandoned by life and love. And that's by softening into the stillness and letting the storylines float by. Become open and spacious like the sky and you will find that you are not alone because *God is always with you.* Polish the mirror of your consciousness and you will see that the Beloved is *right here*

The best gift you can give not only to yourself but also to your partner is to allow relationship to be a vehicle for emotional and spiritual growth.

in your own heart. Touch the core of your being and you will find that you are always absolutely whole and complete ... *exactly* as you are right now!

In embracing your aloneness and bringing this into relationship, you move beyond co-dependency to inter-dependency. Instead of relating as two needy children you meet each other in the fullness of your essential maleness and femaleness. It's the dance of these core male and female energies that gives relationship its dynamism and creative power. In inter-dependency, not only do you meet each other as man and woman but also as god and goddess. And in this meeting, the alchemy of true love can take place.

Healing the Male-Female Wound

Embodying the full depth of your essence as a man or as a woman, you transform the unconsciousness that gets played out both in relationship and in the world. This realization has been the single most important factor in changing my experience of life from pain to joy. After many years of playing the victim, I finally worked out what it means to be empowered within intimate relationship. And what a gift this is to the world!

For a man this means embodying the masculine principle of Truth. In its fullness, Truth is experienced as *awareness* or depth of *presence*. It's like a sword of light that penetrates each moment to illuminate the stark naked reality of *what is*. Of course, it's not always as clear as that! Awareness can be clouded over by layers of conditioning. But whether the blade is sharp or blunt, the sword of awareness is always one-pointed. It's why men are easily absorbed in doing something, such as watching football, surfing the web, collecting stamps or investing in stocks and shares. And why they are mostly able to concentrate on only one thing at a time! It's also why they tend to have a mission in life that they follow with great zeal.

Transformation through love can only happen when we are willing to let go of everything. And this includes our fear of being alone.

Underlying this single-minded pursuit is a man's natural thirst for freedom. By losing himself in sex, drugs and rock'n'roll or in never-ending deadlines at work or even in the solitude of meditation, he seeks to free himself from the nagging discontent of false self. But how free a man actually becomes depends on how conscious he is. If he's not conscious, he remains in a horizontal reality and loses himself in external activities in order to shut off his true feelings.

A man's road to freedom is not to move away from himself but to move even deeper inside himself. Whatever he is doing – whether mowing the lawn or reciting mantras – it is only by being totally present in his body, his mind and his emotions that he starts the process of dis-identification with small self. By diving deep into the verticality of each moment as it arises, he discovers that beneath the fleeting nature of all sensations, thoughts and feelings is the eternal emptiness of his Being-nature.

In relationship, this means that a man can transform the unconsciousness within him by being in touch with his truth. By being authentic in everything he says and does, he can stay present with his partner, he can take responsibility for his feelings, be honest, and have the courage to be vulnerable. Only when a man stops looking outside of himself for freedom and instead immerses himself in the truth of *this* moment as it unfolds can he truly relate. And only then can he fulfill his true purpose which is to shine as the god he truly is.

A man who fulfills his true purpose of living his truth and brings this into relationship allows a woman to fulfill her true purpose of surrender. Every woman embodies the feminine principle of Love. In its fullness, Love is experienced as an emanation of *light*, an unbounded *radiance* that spills out from an overflowing bowl to enchant everything it touches. It's why women have a natural inclination to spread their energy outwards. You can see how multi-tasking comes easily to them and why they enjoy sharing their time, space and resources. It could be baking cakes for the whole family or surrounding themselves with children or offering a listening ear at times of crisis. Or just gossiping with friends.

Underlying this is woman's natural state of devotion. She yearns to give herself totally ... whether it is to her lover, to her children, to her guru or to a worthy cause. But how tainted this love is by the needs of small self depends on how conscious she is. If she's not conscious, she gives of herself so that she may be loved in return. In the horizontal dimension, her love is conditional because she fears abandonment.

It's in giving herself up to her aloneness that woman finds the fulfillment she seeks. By surrendering deeply to Life *as it is*, her love becomes selfless. In the vertical dimension, her love is unconditional. As she opens ever-more deeply and allows her true radiance to pour forth, she no longer needs someone to love: she simply *is* love. And her beauty is no longer skin-deep but arises from her depths as the eternal glow of Being.

The power to stay open as unbounded love is woman's true power. And when she brings this into relationship she can transform the unconsciousness within it. By staying open through all the tears, rage and howling pain without fear of abandonment she devotes herself to that which is greater than small self. And in giving herself willingly to the aloneness of her essential nature, she relates as the goddess she truly is.

One of the gifts of my relationship with Kavi is that his devotion to the truth of *this* moment allows me to absolutely trust him. Even when the truth means his ego takes a battering, he does it with grace. It means I can always trust him to put

God above all else. And that means I can let go of trying to fix him, change him or hold onto him. Instead, I can let go into *this* moment and know that God will take care of all the details.

When man faces woman in Truth and woman opens to him as Love, there's a magic that happens that heals the age-old rift between male and female. When you stop going to war with each other, you can literally make love. And the more love you make, the more there is to share. Instead of a battleground, your relationship becomes a vehicle for universal healing. It is then able to hold not only you, but also each other ... *and* something even greater than both of you together. Frequently this manifests as a common purpose, a vision that you share or your life's work together. It could be raising a family in love and consciousness or building an ethical business or offering your services to others.

Bringing Love and Truth to *every* aspect of your relationship transforms the struggle of human love to the blessing of Divine Love. When the veil lifts, you see that God has been hiding right before your very eyes. Beholding the Beloved in your beloved is truly one of the most healing and liberating experiences!

Entering the Gateway of Relationship

If you wish to deepen your experience of relationship, you may want to try out this simple but powerful exercise. Not only does it bring you closer to your partner but it also helps you enter the gateway of relationship to God. You can also do this without a partner, simply by gazing into your own eyes in a mirror.

Start off by sitting opposite your partner in a comfortable position. Cross-legged is good as it's best to be close enough to see clearly into each other's eyes. Take a few deep, conscious breaths to relax your body and to help you become more fully present. Now gently gaze into each other's eyes and keep breathing consciously and softly. Long, slow breaths, in through the nose and out through the mouth. Remember to keep it soft and slow - you don't want to hyperventilate!

As you do this for several minutes, you will most probably feel like saying something or even feel like turning away. Resist the temptation to speak, to move or to stop! Simply watch the discomfort arising. If tears or laughter happen, then let them. But keep breathing and gazing. Undoubtedly

When man faces woman in Truth and woman opens to him as Love, there's a magic that happens that heals the age-old rift between male and female.

you will experience all sorts of feelings, emotions and thoughts, some more pleasant than others. Allow yourself to feel vulnerable, to be seen by the other. Simply allow whatever judgment, fear, repulsion, attraction or any sensation to float by. Watch how all these thoughts and feelings come and go, how they are impermanent.

Stay with this process for at least 10 minutes, if not 15 or 20. As you keep gazing into each other's eyes, you will notice that your partner's face changes. It may go through several transformations from ugliness to beauty, from hardness to softness, or from youthfulness to old age. You may see characteristics in your partner you have never been aware of before, fleeting energies that surprise you. Don't get attached to these. Just keep gazing softly and breathing.

If you stay open to whatever it is you are experiencing, you will see beyond the mask of personality that hides the true nature of your partner. You will see that part of him or her that is eternal; you will see his or her Being nature. Instead of seeing with your eyes, you will see with your heart.

And when two hearts meet, you come face to face with God ... and realize that all separation is an illusion.

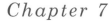

Chapter 7

MANIFESTING YOUR DESTINY: *The Gateway of the World*

This gateway is a big one! So bedazzled are we by the world and its many marvels – and its many horrors too – that we very often forget what we are here on Earth to do.

The world can be both exciting and terrifying, we may feel fascinated by it or repulsed by it, we may want to explore it, conquer it, tame it or hide from it. It has given birth to empires, cultures and traditions as varied as the colors of the rainbow. It has seen the flowering of science, art and education, the explosion of agriculture, industry and technology, and witnessed the rise and fall of social structures and ideologies. Whichever way we look at it, we cannot help but be held captive by its sheer magnitude and complexity. It is probably not surprising that in the face of such a colossal force we easily lose our own stature and become but pale reflections of who we really are.

We forget that we are here to shine the light of our magnificence on everything we say and do, that we are here to know the truth of our infinite potential. We forget that we are here to remember our divinity and to manifest our destiny. It does not serve us to shrink at the awesome power of the world nor to pit ourselves against it as if it were the enemy. This neither helps us nor does it help the world. Each of us has access to a wealth of creative energy. We can choose to tap into it, live our purpose and offer our gifts to the world or we can play it small and convince ourselves that

If we truly understood that the outer world is a reflection of our inner world, we would realize how absolutely powerful we are.

resources – both inner and outer – are in short supply. It is only by daring to be all that we can be that we enrich our lives and those of others. It is only by showing the world our true worth that the world repays us in riches beyond our wildest dreams.

If we truly understood that the outer world is a reflection of our inner world, we would realize how absolutely powerful we are. And we would remember that we are here to recreate the world just as we want it.

Is It Really a Big Bad World Out There?

These days, there's no avoiding the news. Every day we hear about another murder that saddens us, another racial attack that angers us, another political scandal that rocks our faith in world leadership, and yet another natural disaster that shakes the foundations of our global community. Every day 25,000 people die of starvation, over 100,000 acres of rainforest are destroyed, and 137 plant and animal species become extinct. Today, I sat down and cried my eyes out when I read that an estimated 200 million animals are slaughtered – under inhumane conditions – per day in order to provide us with meat. That's 200 million per day! Can you believe it?

Faced with such information, how can we fail to believe it's a Big Bad World out there? How can we not believe that "the world is in a terrible mess and there's nothing I can do about it?" What we fail to realize is that the world is in such a terrible mess precisely *because* we believe there's nothing we can do about it!

We have misplaced our inner authority and forgotten that we are in fact the authors of our own reality. In believing that we are powerless, we have become powerless. In allowing an external authority to tell us what is right and what is wrong we have built a huge wall between Us and Them. The collective forces of politics, economics, mass media and culture appear to be so great that we may wonder what choice we have other than to quietly conform. Or perhaps to rebel. Yet neither of these options give us the result we really want.

Campaigning for justice, fighting the good cause, overthrowing the oppressors or eradicating the enemy might make us feel that we are doing something useful but they simply exacerbate an already inflamed situation. It's like fighting fire with fire: it just makes things worse! Today, there's the war on drugs, the war on crime, the war on famine and the war on global warming. And then there's the war on terrorism. So adamant are we that we are right and they are wrong that we are willing to attack, destroy and perform all kinds of atrocities against those who appear to be the problem. And so the world divides: nation against nation; villains versus victims; good versus bad. Surely we're missing the point here? I'm certainly not suggesting we stick our heads in the sand and pretend everything's just fine. There have been some incredible milestones made for

*By judging or hating the world for being imperfect, we create the very thing we judge or hate. There **is** no Big Bad World out there, only a reflection of where we cast the darkness of our unloving thoughts.*

freedom and equality by individuals who've had the courage to stand up and speak the truth. But as Gandhi said: "An eye for an eye and the whole world goes blind."

I was told a story once, about how God created the world and asked all his angels to love His Creation as much as they loved Him. They all agreed except for one who said that he loved God with all his heart but could not possibly love the world in the same way because nothing was as exalted as God. So God repeated his request that all the angels love the world as much as they loved Him. And again they all agreed except for the one angel who could not possibly love the world as much as he loved God. And so God reluctantly expelled this angel from the Kingdom of Heaven. It is said that this is how Satan came into existence. The Devil is nothing more than a fallen angel, one who is blind to the holiness of the world. In refusing to see God and His Creation as one and the same, he succumbs to the illusion of separation and tumbles from the perfection of Paradise into a horizontal reality of fear and limitation.

The meaning of the story is clear: *every* aspect of the world is an expression of God's will. The only evil that exists is the part of *us* that does not embrace the world in its fullness. By judging or hating the world for being imperfect, we create the very thing we judge or hate. There *is* no Big Bad World out there, only a reflection of where we cast the darkness of our unloving thoughts.

The only real conspiracy is the one in your head. And the only revolution worth making is the one in your heart. We heal the world, not by fighting it, but by illuminating it with the brightness of our love.

The Joy of Becoming a Co-Creator

We are all born with an innate drive to live our true purpose, to manifest our highest potential and to be fully empowered. It's part of the ever-unfolding evolutionary plan. It's what engages us with the process of creative growth and expansion. And it's what makes life interesting.

But the power we seek is not to be found in the external world. All our attempts to fix it, control it, make it better, to get more success, more money, more status, more possessions, more this or more that are doomed to failure. When we are dependent on external circumstances for our sense of power then we are at the mercy of the tides of change. Everything fluctuates; everything grows into fullness and then returns to emptiness. Even the most seemingly powerful things in the world are subject to this basic law of birth and death. Just as a mountain eventually erodes to dust, so does a millionaire die with nothing.

The only power we truly have is the power to choose love over fear. This one choice gives us the power to create our reality. You can see how powerful this is when you look at the world we live in today. It is no accident that violence, war, struggle and scarcity are the dominant themes. The vast majority of human thinking is dominated by fearful thoughts.

The point really hit home when I heard Marianne Williamson speak with passionate eloquence about how it is that a handful of terrorists have terrorized the world. It is because they have absolute conviction in their hatred: they don't hate *some* of the time but *all* of the time. If only we could love with the same conviction, the world would change overnight!

The universal Law of Attraction states that we are all magnets and we attract to ourselves whatever matches

The only power we truly have is the power to choose love over fear. This one choice gives us the power to create our reality.

our vibrational frequency. Ultimately, there are only two frequencies in Existence: fear and love. When we focus on what we *don't* like or *don't* want, we vibrate to the frequency of fear. When you watch the news on TV and react in anger, revenge or blame, then you are simply adding to the hatred in the world. When you read the daily papers and feel depressed, insecure and helpless, you are simply adding to the despair in the world. We cannot and should not turn a blind eye to the world's suffering. But giving our attention to negativity simply adds to it and keeps us locked in victimhood.

It is only when we choose the openness of love that our world changes from one of limitation to one of infinite possibilities. We transform our reality by giving our attention to thoughts of abundance, gratitude, happiness and peace. Deep in our hearts we know this. That's why movies such as *Groundhog Day* make such an impression on us. I don't think any other film has captured the shift from horizontal to vertical reality in such an accessible yet poignant way.

In this film Bill Murray plays an egocentric weather-reporter doomed to live out the same day of his life repeatedly. At first, he is his usual grumpy and cynical self. But as time goes by and he comes to know what to expect from his day, he becomes depressed. He even tries to kill himself to relieve the monotony. Eventually he succumbs to his fate and attempts to get the most out of it. He turns his attention to impressing a female co-worker in order to boost his self-esteem. But all his attempts to get her into bed backfire and he's left miserable again.

Finally, when he realizes that he is trapped in the eternal *now*, something snaps in him and he decides to do only the things that he really enjoys. Instead of searching for self-gratification he turns to learning new creative skills and doing good deeds just for the sheer joy of it. The more he opens to Life *as it is*, the more he feels grateful for the little things that happen to him. When he finally becomes a genuinely loving person, his life is transformed. Not only does the beautiful woman he had given up chasing fall in love with him but the spell of the ever-repeating day is broken. In the final scene, he literally wakes up to a new day bursting with sunshine and fresh beginnings.

What this wonderful story shows is how when we push against the world because we want things to be different, we end up in a self-perpetuating cycle of misery. Whereas when we innocently follow our bliss – regardless of outcome or personal agenda – we are guided towards our divine destiny. Bliss – or joy – is of the highest vibration and aligns us to God's will so that we become conscious co-creators of our world. We cannot fake joy: it is a state of being born from genuine appreciation for what we *do* like and *do* want. Joy and gratitude go hand in hand. And wherever they go, grace is bound to follow.

When you love what you do and do what you love, doors open and miracles happen.

Bliss – or joy – is of the highest vibration and aligns us to God's will so that we become conscious co-creators of our world.

Loving the Work You Do and Doing the Work You Love

For many of us, work is something we have to endure rather than something we enjoy. It's something we have to do in order to make ends meet or to give us the lifestyle we aspire to. Sometimes it's something we do because it gives us a sense of identity or a certain position in the world. But when we are struggling to survive in a job that barely pays the bills or carving out a career so that we have security and status, work becomes a means to an end and it is diminished to a horizontal experience. In the long term, this fails to nourish us on a soul level.

Surveys into work attitudes show that most people believe they should do as little as they can for as much money as they can and then get home as early as they can! Let's be honest here, would you work if you didn't have to? How much time do you spend planning for the weekend when you can have some fun with family and friends? Or daydreaming about that special holiday? Or maybe fantasizing about all the things you can do when you retire? Considering that work takes up such a vast proportion of our waking life, that's a lot of energy wasted resisting what's happening right here and now. No wonder most of us equate work with effort and struggle! If we're not feeling anxious, tense and pressured, then we're feeling resentful, frustrated and bored. And then after a day's work we expect to go home and be relaxed and loving!

Some of us even believe we can live a spiritual life – perhaps participating in transformational courses, going to yoga classes or meditating daily – whilst harboring deep-seated negativity about work. But how can you be truly spiritual when you spend 85 percent of your time hating your job? The problem with holding a belief that says work is something you have to grin and bear whilst love and laughter is what happens in whatever time you have left over, is that it splits you in two. But if you are on a path of awakening, you cannot love life part-time. It's all or nothing when it comes to liberation!

I'm often asked what it takes to stay motivated when there's no-one to wield the stick at work. Being my own boss, of course, I have to set my own goals and guidelines almost on a daily basis. Certainly, a fair dose of discipline is required. But motivation is not the issue here. Having to be motivated implies you have your sights on the end result. That's great for kick-starting a project or making plans to turn your dream into a reality, but eventually your batteries will run dry. The way I see it, what's important is being *total*. Being total means you are fully present, *wherever* you are and *whatever* you are doing. Love for what you do is the only motivation that really works in the long run.

Work is an integral part of today's spiritual path and it will pay huge dividends if you get conscious of your relationship to it. So often we carry our smallness into our work environment, hiding our true light behind self-limiting beliefs. And then we wonder why we feel like something is missing. Somehow it's easier to blame our boss, our parents, our schooling, our society or our karma for our unhappiness rather than take full responsibility for where we are. Getting conscious of your relationship to your work means being ruthlessly honest with yourself about what keeps you in your current job if you don't like it. Is it money, recognition, security, family expectation? Maybe it's desperation? And then it means getting clear about what you really want. Is it money, recognition, security, approval? And if so, then what's underneath that? Is it the need to feel loved? Or do you really want purposefulness, a sense of community, to be of service, to spread love? And most importantly, what is it you really enjoy?

By bringing to light unconscious beliefs about your relationship to work, you change your inner reality and can transform even the most humdrum of jobs. It's not *what* you do but *how* you do it that matters! Inner fulfillment – and outer success – come from the willingness to step out of victimhood and into the totality of *this* moment. If you love the work you do, not only will you feel nourished but you will bring a new level of excellence to it. Whilst you may not be able to single-handedly change the way a soulless profit-oriented corporation does business, you can shine at what you do by offering your love on a moment-to-moment basis. If each of us had the courage to be the brightest we could be, if we dared to reveal our authentic presence at all times and in every circumstance, then work would transform from a competitive ego-driven arena in which there are winners and losers to an atmosphere of co-operation in which everyone benefits.

And now I'm going to say something that is, perhaps, radical: if you can't love the work you do, then don't do it!

I'm suggesting taking a risk and trusting that Existence will support you. This might mean doing part-time work whilst you go on an inner journey to find out what it is that you do love doing. Or it might mean being unemployed whilst you develop your inner resources to allow your true light to shine forth into the world. When finding your soul's purpose becomes your top priority then all the angels celebrate and gather round to give you all the help you are willing to receive.

Many years ago, when I left my burgeoning academic career to follow a deeper calling, I had no idea what I would be doing next. It was like stepping into a void and it took every ounce of courage to trust an inner voice that told me it would be OK. I spent several years doing nothing and despite reaching a point of destitution I always felt supported by an invisible force. Even though this period of my life was incredibly difficult, I have always honored it as an invaluable gestation time that allowed me to turn my perspective around from me-centered careerism to God-centered service.

The shift that transforms your reality is from asking God to do things for you to asking God what you can do for *Him*! Instead of asking for more money, power, security or

*Inner fulfillment – and outer success – come from the willingness to step out of victimhood and into the totality of **this** moment.*

approval, ask Him how best you can express your unique talents so that the world's vibration is lifted by Love. When we change our perception from taking to giving, we enter the vertical dimension and transform a chore to a creative expression of God's will. There is no greater joy than this, for whenever we are aligned to Divine Will we are being true to ourselves.

These days, when I ask myself what I can do to serve the world, there is no confusion. There is absolutely no debate. It's a question I ask myself many times and the answer always reveals itself as the unquestionable truth of an uncluttered heart. My job is to simply be as total as I can in this and every moment ... *whatever* I am doing.

Offering Your Gifts to the World

What the world wants more than anything else is your authenticity. When you drop your storylines of "not being good enough to offer what you really love doing" and instead allow your passion to guide you, then you will find your rightful place in the world.

Each of us has something special to offer, something that so perfectly fits in with Divine Plan that to withhold it from the world would be like trying to prevent a beautiful flower from growing. There's no "higher" or "lower" job description in God's eyes, just as there is no "better" or "worse" in the natural world: the roots of a lotus that dwell in muddy darkness at the bottom of a lake are as blessed as the glorious petals that reach for the sunlight. Whether you are a mother, a road-sweeper, an artist, a visionary, or a corporate manager, everything is holy when it is an expression of your honest passion. It is only when we deviate from our authenticity that what we do becomes less than sacred.

Being authentic opens up an infinite source of creative energy that has the ability to fulfill our deepest desires as well as the power to nourish the world. It is inspiration that brings you all the success and wealth that you need, not greed or cunning or sheer hard work. Inspiration is a higher form of motivation. It arises out of the unadulterated joy of Being. People complain that they are full of good ideas but don't feel inspired to act on them or that they want to be creative but don't feel inspired enough to get started. But there is no point waiting to be inspired: it's a form of procrastination that only serves to keep you small. Just be absolutely present and absolutely yourself and inspiration will fill you as surely as the next breath you take fills your lungs.

When you operate from joy rather than duty, you are inspired and you are an inspiration to others. There's a raising of your vibrational frequency that draws to you exactly what you need. It doesn't matter whether it is thousands who are touched by your vision or just one. What matters is that you have been lifted out of self-centeredness and into God's lap. There's nothing more contagious than someone who is both enthused by their vision and deeply relaxed as themselves. Add to this an enthusiasm to share this vision with others and you have a ripple of excitement that is almost palpable. I know that, for myself, if I'm not excited by what I am doing or saying then I'm off on the wrong track.

God wants your highest good: it is only your ego that stands in the way. Small self will put up endless excuses for not doing something. How much easier it is to hide in the shadows of smallness than to stand in the glaring spotlight of the world. The journey of offering your gifts requires you to step out of your imaginary safety zone and stretch your boundaries. It's a risk because you have to be prepared for failure, loss, disappointment, obstacles and uncertainty. These may not necessarily happen but being open to the possibility means you grow in spiritual wealth. In staying softly open when you come up against a hard edge of fear, you release the ego's identification with either success or failure, with either gain or loss, and uncover the eternal jewel of your true nature.

A few years ago, when my "personal transformation" teaching business that I had lovingly nurtured over seven years dissolved to dust, I saw it as a great lesson in non-attachment. Whilst I grieved for what had gone, I also knew that who I really am has nothing to do with my role as teacher or businesswoman. Knowing myself as the unchanging is-ness that underpins it all has allowed me to move on with graciousness.

You have to dig deep to recognize your true worth. Only then will the world recognize you as who you were born to be. When you are generous with your gifts the world will repay you with all the riches you require. God's world is eternally abundant. And so are you ... if only you would recognize it.

Raising the Money Vibration

One of humanity's deepest wounds is about money. We have a firmly embedded belief that money and God do not go together! Tradition has taught us that the more spiritual we are, the less material wealth we should have. Think of Mother Teresa or the Dalai Lama and you inevitably get a picture of someone who has renounced all earthly possessions. Think of monks, nuns, saints and holy men and you immediately get the impression that purity and poverty are synonymous.

God knows I've swallowed this lie ever since I modeled myself on the Virgin Mary at the age of three! Of course, I was totally unaware of this. Like most people, I grew up wanting nice things and dreamed of being rich. But somehow, the closer I got to God, the less money I had! There's so much guilt, shame, fear and judgment that corrupts our relationship to money. For years I felt terribly uncomfortable charging a nominal fee for my healing services. Somehow helping people on their spiritual path and being rewarded financially didn't make easy bedfellows!

It's taken me a long time to figure out that money is neither intrinsically good nor bad: money is neutral! Money is simply a current of energy that responds to our state of consciousness. The true value of money is not the numbers we assign to it but our own internal value system that we project onto it. If we derive our sense of self from the size of our bank balance, then we are not valuing that which we truly are. When we look outside ourselves for our sense of worth, we are more likely to sacrifice the tender honesty of love for the hard evidence of cash and all that it can buy.

This is what is meant by Jesus's statement that it is harder for a rich man to enter Heaven than for a camel to walk through the eye of a needle. It's not that money is bad: rather it's our distorted relationship to it that creates corruption. It is ego's belief in separation that creates a world divided into excessive wealth and abject poverty, a world in which material riches are idolized at the expense of spiritual worth, a world in which crime pays but love doesn't. In the hands of unconsciousness, money is tainted and becomes a vehicle for exploitation.

One of the most important things we can do to heal our world is to heal our relationship to money. I never thought I'd say this, but I now realize that money in the hands of consciousness has the power to cure the world's ills. Imagine a world in which the only purpose of money was to serve Love, a world in which vast reservoirs of wealth were channeled into those areas that have been deprived for so long, that instead of Profit At All Cost the motto for business would be For The Benefit Of All Humankind. Imagine a world in which resources were shared equally, creative enterprise was actively supported and everyone had access to whatever they needed to fulfill their highest potential.

The redistribution of global wealth is Love in Action. It's a much more powerful agent of change than getting stuck in resenting those who have more than you or wallowing in self-justified poverty. We can start the process of change by having a good look at our own beliefs around money. We need an honest examination of our fears, our wounds, and our stubborn adherence to scarcity-consciousness. We need to

Money is simply a current of energy that responds to our state of consciousness.

come clean and be transparent in all our monetary dealings. So often we lie to others and to ourselves about how we use money: over-spending, impulse buying, uncontrollable debt, stinginess, hoarding, messy accounting ... all these are symptoms not only of unconscious money management but also of how we mismanage our internal resources.

A wise man once urged me to gamble everything for Love and Truth, to invest in my long-range joy not my short-term needs. He told me that the more I gave away without concern for small self, the more I would receive from Universal Abundance.

I believe that as more and more people awaken and collective consciousness moves into the eternal *now*, this investment will show an immediate return. When money is given and received unconditionally, it becomes energetically cleansed. Now imagine if each of us would become an agent of "spiritual money laundering!" Would the world not be a brighter place? I believe the future of our species – and the future of our planet – depends on it!

Entering the Gateway of the World

I invite you now to take a deep breath and go inside. Rest for a few moments in the center of your chest. Breathe gently and allow yourself to enter a space of silence and stillness. Take all the time you need until you are ready to go a little deeper. And now rest in your belly, let's say a few centimeters above your navel. Breathe here softly and relax, taking all the time you need.

And again – when you are ready – on your next in-breath imagine drawing in the warmth of the sun, soft golden rays gently penetrating your body and being. With each in-breath allow this golden glow to grow and envelop you in luxurious waves of warm energy. And with each out-breath send this energy back out again into the space around you.

Spend as long as you like breathing in and out like this. As you breathe in, feel yourself expand and vibrate as a golden ball of light. And each time you breathe out, multiply the energy and send it out into the world as waves of bliss and joy. It's as if you are now the sun at the center, pulsating with golden life-force and sending rays of soft, strong warmth in all directions.

Now imagine the whole world is energized by this golden light that keeps flowing into your belly and out again. Imagine everything you say, do or think is immersed in glittering, golden light. Imagine everyone you meet is touched by it and everything you touch is transformed by it. Every interaction you have creates a smile and every transaction you make turns to gold. Imagine this wave of transformation – set in motion simply by your intention – travels around the globe and gets passed on from person to person. Until the whole world is set alight by the spark of your inner divinity.

Imagine everyone and everything glitters with majestic abundance. Imagine the whole world is a jewel of infinite beauty and unquantifiable worth. Now isn't this a world worth inhabiting?

Chapter 8

LOVING THE EARTH:
The Gateway of the Planet

Step back a few thousand miles from where you are now and you'll find yourself looking at a small blue sphere pulsating with an aura of undeniable brilliance and glowing with a breathtaking beauty. This is Earth. The gateway of the planet may seem like a world away from the immediacy of human affairs but our very survival depends on our ability to sense the heartbeat beneath our feet. Far from being an inanimate lump of rock hurtling through space, the planet we live on is as alive as you and me.

This luminescent biosphere is born of the marriage of

In deep communion with Nature you arrive at the inner sanctum of the global heart.

matter and spirit and the fecundity of Nature is an expression of cosmic lovemaking. Everywhere we look is evidence of the exquisitely orchestrated dance of *yin* and *yang*. From the tiniest bud waiting to burst into full bloom to the raging inferno of a volcano about to erupt; and from the bounciest lambs born into the innocence of springtime to the gnarled grandeur of a giant oak tree hundreds of years old, we see God's primordial passion unveiled in myriad forms.

Pick any one of these living forms and you will discover a portal to Universal Love. In deep communion with Nature you arrive at the inner sanctum of the global heart. Watch the sun set slowly over the horizon with unwavering presence and you are likely to experience the timelessness of ecstasy. Listen to the chatter of birdsong with an uncensoring ear and you will probably hear the sweet sound of silence. And sit long enough with a quiet mind by a bubbling stream and you will undoubtedly be immersed in stillness. Simply being with Nature in openness takes you beyond skin-encapsulated ego into the unboundedness of *All That Is*.

In the realization of our oneness, we cannot help but fall in love with every detail of God's earthly garden of delights. It's a love affair that may well be our only saving grace.

The Biggest Blunder We've Ever Made

We've made a terrible mistake. We've lost sight of the Earth as a living, breathing organism. We've mined her resources, cut down her trees, slaughtered her animals, dumped our rubbish, and messed up the atmosphere. We've plundered and polluted without a care in the world. Until now.

We have to face facts: the effects of global warming are potentially catastrophic. Sea levels are rising, ice caps are melting, vast expanses of land are turning into desert, unprecedented number of flora and fauna are dying, the weather is becoming dangerously unpredictable and the ozone layer is disappearing fast. The truth is as inconvenient as it is shocking! Earth is our home. And if we don't wake up to a broader vision soon, we may well find ourselves homeless.

We are being called to get conscious of our relationship to the planet we inhabit. And this means becoming aware of our self-centeredness. How much easier it is to take as much as we can without a thought for what we can give back. Do we really think we can keep on feathering our own nests whilst the world's resources dwindle down to zero? Or that we can allow just 10 percent of the world's population to own 90 percent of the world's wealth? It's not just a matter of becoming ecologically hip; it's much deeper than that. It's about admitting our allegiance to ego instead of to God. We're guilty of instant gratification regardless of the cost to future generations. We've chosen to see the planet as a commodity rather than as a manifestation of the divine. It's akin to rape, and there's a price to pay.

But there's no point wallowing in self-recrimination. Nor is there any point waiting for the environmentalists to clean it all up or for major corporations to have an epiphany on trading policies or for the Green Party to get a majority vote. It's not a social or a political matter: it's a spiritual one. It's up to each one of us to open our eyes – and our hearts – to the miracle of God's creation. Do we really believe that we stand apart from the rest of Existence? Or could we stretch our imaginations a little to see that all living things are interconnected? Are we really numb to the enormity of environmental devastation? Or can we soften a little to feel the pangs of planetary pain seeping into our everyday lives?

Our challenge is to stay open amidst the stark reality of potential planetary destruction. The strength of our storylines is enormous here. How much easier it is to rage against the machine of modernization than to simply be present to Life *as it is now*! How much more convenient to retreat into hopelessness than to risk the agony of a broken heart if it all goes wrong!

Several years ago I decided I would turn my back on civilization and run to the hills, build an eco-house and become totally self-sufficient in order to survive the impending apocalypse. Of course, I didn't do it and I'm still here. Time and maturity have given me a different perspective and I realized that converting to solar power and growing my own vegetables won't make an iota of difference if self-preservation is my primary motive.

Saving the planet needs to arise out of love not fear. It

is not so much the changes we make on the physical plane that matter but the changes we make on the inner plane. When we are willing to make the transition from personal to universal consciousness then all our actions will be aligned to the planet's welfare. We need to be ruthlessly honest with ourselves as we go about our ecological campaign. For example, do you recycle with resentment? Do you judge those who drive gas-guzzling 4x4s? Even the merest hint of a storyline attached to your green-conscious actions will prevent you from making the leap from a horizontal to a vertical reality. I know it sounds harsh but nothing less than total commitment to conscious living is required if we are to enter the gateway of the planet. It's no longer wise to ignore the winds of change, to blindly go about our lives as

Saving the planet needs to arise out of love not fear. It is not so much the changes we make on the physical plane that matter but the changes we make on the inner plane.

if nothing is happening. There's too much to lose ... and so much to gain!

These turbulent times may well be the greatest opportunity we have for collective transformation. By facing our current crisis with the full depth of our presence and the full breadth of our openness we may actually see how our belief in separation is a lie that we can no longer afford to uphold. We just might see once and for all that you, me, the rest of humanity and every single thing that lives and breathes – including the planet – is deeply connected.

We just might wake up and realize that we *are all one*.

Compassion for Gaia

Creation is made up of energy. From the stars in the sky to the soil beneath our feet and from the air that we breathe to the blood in our veins, we are all made up of the same stuff. Existence is consciousness in a variety of manifestations. Everything – from an elephant to an amoeba and from a mountain to a molecule – has consciousness to one degree or another. Where there is life, there is energy. And where

Earth is more than just our home: Earth is our Mother.

there is energy, there is consciousness. All life is connected because all life originates from the same source.

We don't need science to tell us this – even though modern physics shows us that the Universe is created out of one vibrating energy field – because when our hearts are open and we are deeply rooted in *this* moment we feel it in our bones. Earth is more than just our home: Earth is our Mother. We have been created by her and we are supported by her intricate ecosystem. We are an intrinsic part of her and the connection stretches over eons to create a common ancestry for all human beings and all living things. We are related to every animal, tree, plant, river and stone that has ever existed. Our spiritual roots are deeply embedded in the Earth.

Ancient cultures knew this and honored her as Gaia, the Great Goddess that gives birth to all life forms. But somewhere along the line, there's been a collective amnesia. We've unplugged ourselves from the cosmic pulse and taken

We are related to every animal, tree, plant, river and stone that has ever existed.

up residence in the confines of our heads. And now heart and mind are disconnected. It's like a relationship in which communication has broken down.

The masculine principle of logic and linear thinking has stopped listening to the feminine voice of intuition and subtle feeling and has turned its single-mindedness to the relentless pursuit of technological advance. The masculine has become like a hero on a mission, ruthlessly cutting down trees and digging into the Earth, building more roads, more factories and more housing, conquering the highest mountains and exploring outer space in the quest for dominion over his habitat. In the meantime, the feminine principle, rooted in the earthly realm of rhythmical flow and natural cycles is crying out for attention. And just as an unfulfilled woman becomes over-emotional and needy, so the planet is exhibiting erratic behavior. The unprecedented increase in the number of devastating hurricanes, heatwaves and floods over the past few decades across the globe is no coincidence. It's clear that the collective masculine and feminine energies are severely out of balance and it's making our planet sick.

It seems to me that humanity's hero needs to find his heart again. The hero lives inside each of us, not just in men, although he's more obvious here. The hero is that part of us that loves adventure and strives for perfection and peak performance. The danger is that this forward-thrusting part of us gets lost in doing and forgets to rest in the simplicity of Being. It reminds me of the myth of Parsifal who, as a young boy, leaves home to become a knight. There are many variations of the story but the overall theme is the same.

Parsifal's naivety and innocence turn to courage and strength as he travels far and wide, overcoming danger and amassing glory and great riches. One day, as he falls asleep, exhausted from the most recent conquest, he experiences a vision in which he enters a glittering castle and meets a wounded king who tells him how the land is dying through neglect. He also meets a beautiful maiden who holds out to him the most precious prize of all: the Holy Grail, a dazzling stone with magical powers. But Parsifal stands there speechless, not knowing what to do and the vision fades.

When he awakens, he feels strangely desolate and vows to find this mysterious palace again.

It is only after many years of trial and tribulation that he rediscovers the palace. This time, he has the maturity and wisdom to see beyond the glitter and to contemplate the deeper meaning of the Holy Grail. Instead of trying to work out what he should do with it, he looks within and asks himself how best he can serve such divine beauty. This simple shift in attention is a profound one in which the masculine comes into right relationship with the feminine.

Parsifal's story ends with him becoming the custodian of the Holy Grail, an honor that deeply humbles him. The final piece of the jigsaw is put into place when he also realizes that he is the king's son, the maiden is to be his wife and the castle is his inheritance. In acceptance of these gifts, he reawakens to his rightful role, the king's wound is healed and the land is restored to its bounteousness. Likewise, when we too sacrifice our ego on the altar of that which is greater than us – in other words, God – we heal the split between masculine and feminine and come into wholeness. This is the alchemical marriage that gives birth to our full creative potential and reconnects us to our divine heritage.

When we awaken to our true nature, we reignite the love affair with all that is alive. We remember Earth as the Mother of Creation and we develop deep empathy for all her children. We feel her pain as our own and we do not hesitate to do all we can to alleviate the suffering.

It is not until we develop compassion for Gaia that Earth will be restored to her full glory.

Nature's Secret

Nature is the holder of an ancient wisdom and if we look and listen carefully she will share her secret with us. In allowing our awareness to rest softly and silently with whatever is natural, we are shown a way out of the mess we have created. God has given us a blueprint for personal and planetary well-being and it's made available to us through the tangible world of living form.

Wherever we look in Nature we will see a reflection of our own inner nature. The universe is holographic, so everything that exists provides a snapshot of how things are. This applies both to our collective outer reality as well as to our personal inner reality. The animal, plant and mineral kingdoms as well as the elemental forces all live inside us as well as outside. It makes sense when we remember that as humans we are at the head of our particular evolutionary scale and so we contain within us the genetic and psychic memory of all that has gone before us.

In getting conscious of our relationship to the natural world, we get to see just how far we have strayed from our essential wholeness. All we have to do is look with the eyes of the heart at the animals that run, crawl, swim and fly to see how we are harmed by denial of our raw instinctual nature.

The relatively recent domestication of animals shows us what can happen when we try to control this primal part of us. Animals, which in their normal habitat would be strong and dignified – such as the wild sheep or wild pig – develop quite different characteristics when kept under man-made conditions for successive generations. For example, when I think of a sheep the words "docile" and "stupid" spring to mind and when I think of a pig I get the image of a grubby and bloated specimen! It's a sad reflection of how we have tampered with something naturally beautiful. And what about the mass hunting and farming of wild animals? Surely when we mindlessly captivate and slaughter these untamed creatures, some part of our own wild and free spirit also dies?

From the cold-blooded lizard with its basic survival instinct to the warm-blooded tiger with its fearless intelligence; and from the earth-bound elephant with its memory rooted in the archaic past to the sky-soaring eagle with its eye on the wider perspective, every animal mirrors an aspect of our own psyche. When we disrespect these wonderful life forms, we dishonor ourselves and become less than whole.

There's a rich source of insight in the world of plants too. Contemplate how a tree grows and you'll be shown how to live in harmony with Existence. The roots of a tree reach deep down into the Earth and their branches stretch high up into the sky. We should take note. Balance and strength come from being grounded in reality whilst reaching for the stars. Have you noticed how their dignified serenity allows them to withstand extreme weather conditions, how they stand their ground firmly yet are flexible enough to sway and bend, to go with the flow? Isn't this how we are meant to be? And have you noticed how they bear silent witness to the cycles of time, neither complaining nor retracting? From the bursting forth of new shoots and buds in the spring to

In resting our gaze softly on the Earth, Nature reveals the secret that will save us from destroying ourselves and the planet.

the extravaganza of summer in full bloom through to the colorful shedding of leaves in the autumn and the stark beauty of winter, all are taken in good stride. There is no struggle inherent in the lives of trees. There is only the simple acceptance of what is.

Now contemplate the way a natural forest teems with a rich variety of species. There is no competition here, just a symbiotic relationship, and the result is fertile abundance. But when we control plant growth by artificial methods, forests become denuded and sterile; crops grown with mono-farming methods end up deficient in nutrients. And it's the same with us: too much order in our lives makes us less creative and life loses its zest.

There's a wealth of wisdom beneath the surface of the Earth too. It's here in the underworld that gold can be found, both literally and metaphorically. It's by looking within and embracing ourselves totally that we reclaim our true worth. Surely when we fail to recognize the sacredness of the jewels within the Earth's crust by over-mining, we end up undermining ourselves? Surely when we deny Earth's sanctity by blindly dumping ever-more toxic products back into her body, we upset the delicate balance of all living things including ourselves? Is it any wonder that she threatens to destroy us through ecological upheaval? It's about time we learnt to take only what we really need and to recycle our resources in a safe way. In having less waste, we are less likely to waste away.

In resting our gaze softly on the Earth, Nature reveals the secret that will save us from destroying ourselves and the planet. It's called interdependence. Inside everything that is natural is a sanctuary of sacredness that reminds us of who we are and our place in the bigger scheme of things.

We are here to realize the divinity of all life, to recognize the unity within the diversity. And to know that everything is interconnected by an intricate web of energy that weaves its magic and makes this planet so enchantingly precious.

Reverence and Respect

Resting in the silence of our own inner sanctuary whilst being in a natural environment gives us access to the intelligence of the divine blueprint. But we don't have to live in the wilderness in order to be privy to Nature's teachings. It's a deep knowing in every cell of our beings, an innate wisdom that is available to us when we live deeply and authentically from our essential nature.

I have lived in the inner city of London for most of my life. It is here in the urban jungle that I have attuned to the pulse of Life, to the insistent rhythm of birth, death and rebirth. It is here in the slipstream of the technological highway that I have learnt that the cycles of Nature are the same as my own inner cycles, that nothing really dies but is just recycled and that Life is always in motion.

Like the body of the planet, I too am built of matter, giving me shape, stability and strength from which to plant new creative seeds. Blood courses through my veins just as rivers flow towards the sea and tears soothe my pain just as rain refreshes the land. The heat of the sun is the same as the fire in my belly, igniting my passion and providing the spark for life-sustaining energy. The wind that blows is the same as the air that inspires me, giving my imagination space to soar and clearing both the cobwebs from my mind as well as the debris from ground.

Whilst standing at the edge of a cliff with a vast expanse of unspoilt land unfurling before your eyes is undoubtedly a more transcendent experience than sitting on a park bench watching early morning joggers go by, it's not so much *where* you are as *how* you are that matters. It's the verticality of your vision that defines the depth of your experience. Even a few moments of gentle communion with a houseplant or a shared moment of silent communication with a beloved pet can take you deep into the stillness of Being.

Just one taste of Being is enough to fill you with reverence for Life. Reverence is a sense of wonder at the extraordinary phenomenon of Life. It's a natural response to God's creation, a childlike sense of innocence and trust in the essential goodness of all manifestations.

Reverence sounds serious, but it's not pious. It's prayerful because it fills us with gratitude for the gift of our existence. But it's also playful because it fills us with such delight to play a part in God's evolutionary drama.

What fun we can have knowing that we are co-creators in the unfolding story of Life!

When we have tasted reverence, respect comes naturally. Respect means living in authentic freedom without harm to the greater whole. For example, when somebody carelessly throws rubbish out of a car window they demonstrate a lack of respect towards the Earth. That crisp packet, take-away cup or plastic bag will end up getting blown across the countryside by the wind and will probably go on to poison the soil, pollute a river or choke an animal. Or it just might get caught up in the branches of the tree in my garden and make my immediate environment just a little less attractive.

Imagine what the world would be like if every random act of carelessness was replaced by a random act of kindness? Would we not then inhabit a world of beauty and harmony, a world in which we would respect the sanctity of the planet and revere all living forms as representatives of God?

And imagine if we could travel across the globe in a flash and from our bird's-eye-view see that all the walls we have made out of national identity, cultural tradition, skin color, and religious belief serve to keep us in prison. Would we not bring these walls tumbling down so that we can join hands

Reverence is a sense of wonder at the extraordinary phenomenon of Life.

and rejoice in our oneness? Would our hearts not want to stretch so wide as to place the Earth right in the center and encircle it with a halo of Love?

And wouldn't we want to keep it safe … forever?

Entering the Gateway of the Planet

I'd like to introduce you to the Pink Bubble Meditation. I can't remember where I learnt it or where the name came from, but I've worked with it a lot and it never fails to fill me with compassion for the greater whole.

So perhaps you would join me now. Simply close your eyes, relax your breathing and then bring your awareness to the center of your chest. Breathe in and out here for a while, simply relaxing into the spaciousness of your heart. And on your next in-breath imagine there is a tiny Pink Bubble right here in the center of your heart. And as you breathe out this tiny pink bubble grows a little bigger. Breathe into this pink bubble again and as you breathe out imagine it gets filled up with Love and Light and gets a little bigger.

Each time you breathe in and out this Pink Bubble gets bigger so that it starts to fill up your whole body with Love and Light. Every part of your body and every cell of your being is enveloped in this beautiful Pink Bubble of Unconditional Love and Healing Light. Keep breathing in and out so that the Pink Bubble expands and moves out beyond the boundary of your body. As it fills up with your breath it grows and touches everything in the vicinity ... including all the objects in the room, any other people with you, any plants, any pets and the very air that you breathe.

And let this Pink Bubble expand and move beyond the four walls of your home and out into the surrounding neighborhood to touch and include all the other houses, streets and gardens, all the dogs, all the cats and all the children. Keep breathing and expanding, filling up this Pink Bubble with Unconditional Love and Healing Light, so that it gets bigger and bigger and spreads out into the town or city that you live in and even further out into the countryside. Let it touch and include every tree, every flower and every blade of grass. Let it touch and include all the animals, birds, rivers and stones.

And let this Pink Bubble emanating from the center of your heart expand even more and move out across the land over mountain and sea to touch and include every single thing that exists, across continents and oceans. This Pink Bubble continues to fill with Love and Light until the whole planet is enveloped. Breathe here gently for as long as you like. You and everything that exists is bathed in Unconditional Love and Healing Light. Your heart is as big as the Earth. Global heart. We are all one.

When you are ready – and only then – very slowly draw this Pink Bubble towards you with the Earth and everything that exists still inside it. Draw it towards you so that it gets smaller and smaller. Draw it towards you so that it sits inside the sanctum of your heart.

And now gently reconnect with your breath rising and falling in the center of your chest. When you are ready, open your eyes. Remember as you go about your day that the whole planet and everything on it has a place in the very heart of your being. And that you can return to this sanctuary of stillness and silence whenever you wish.

Chapter 9

DYING INTO GOD:
The Gateway of Spirit

The seventh, and final, gateway is shrouded in mystery. The world of spirit is like a far-away land inhabited by supernatural beings waiting patiently to pamper us and lavish us with love when we finally arrive. Some call it Heaven, Nirvana, Paradise, The Promised Land or Shangri-La. Others call it Transcendence, The Unending State of Bliss, Self-Realization, Samadhi or Enlightenment. But somehow this place is just out of reach, there's always something we need to overcome in order to get there. Or so we're led to believe.

Holy scriptures, esoteric texts, religious leaders, spiritual teachers and new-age gurus tell us we need to abstain, renounce, purify, transcend, practice and do penance. Whether it's meditation, chanting, whirling, cleansing our chakras, fasting or praying, there's always one more thing we need to do before we can be blessed with bliss. And even after many years of diligent practice and austerities, it's not certain that we'll succeed. Perhaps death is the only guarantee of entry to God's abode. And even then stories diverge as to how many lifetimes of trial and error we need to have undergone.

But what if we've been looking in the wrong place? What if God/Spirit/the Divine is not to be found outside of everyday life? What if everything is spiritual exactly *as it is*? And what if the only thing that prevents us from seeing this is our unexamined belief about what, who or where God is?

Could it be that *God is Everything* ... and that *God is Everywhere*? What a revelation! What a glorious celebration Life would be!

Finding God in everything and everywhere reveals your true nature as God. And would God not choose to create Heaven on Earth?

God Has No Religion

For millenia God has been obscured by the dusty veil of religion. Thousands of years of patriarchal rule have seen to it that Our Father/ The Holy Spirit/ Allah/ Yahweh/ Brahman/ The Supreme Being remains out of sight, accessible only via holy texts.

Invariably, these texts tell us that God – by whichever name we choose to call Him – is omnipotent and omniscient. In other words, He is all-powerful and all-knowing. We, on the other hand, are weak and ignorant. We are told that God is The Unquestionable Authority and that He demands obedience. Obeying God's Word – as laid down in a strict code of conduct outlined in the holy texts – gains us entry to Heaven. Disobedience damns us to Hell. Whether we're talking about This Life, the Next Life or the After-Life, beliefs about God all involve the theme of reward and punishment.

Christians are told they only have one life and that when they die God will decide whether they have lived a good life and so will enjoy everlasting peace, or a bad life in which case they'll suffer for eternity. In certain denominations of Christianity it is believed that we are all born as sinners and will go to Hell anyway unless we pray fervently for salvation. Hindus are told that good and bad deeds are accumulated over many lifetimes and union with God can only be achieved when the balance sheet is finally clean. Muslims are given a list of rules to adhere to in daily life and told that any deviation will result in eternal punishment in Hell. Jews believe they have been appointed the Chosen Ones with privileged access to Heaven. Even in Buddhism, there are benevolent and wrathful deities that demand worship.

What an incredibly heavy burden we bear trying to figure out what God really wants and making sure we please Him! It's no surprise we carry so much shame and so much guilt! We have become victims of The Almighty, at the whim of His wrath and His mercy. We blame Him for our misfortunes when things appear to go wrong and are beholden to Him when things appear to go right. No wonder we feel like helpless children waiting for Our Father to protect us from the dangers of life.

But *Stop*! Perhaps we should ask ourselves why it is that in every major religion, God exists outside of us – usually *up there* somewhere – whilst we and Life carry on *down here*. And why it is that the only way we can get to know Him is

In Truth you will see that God is neither a person nor a thing and therefore He does not exist outside of you.

via an intermediary, a Divine Messenger who is chosen to transmit God's Word. We've been told that God only speaks to prophets and priests! Could it be that religion is a pack of storylines that stands in the way of us and God? There's a great joke I found quite by accident on the web the other day in which an Eskimo is having a conversation with a priest. The Eskimo asks: "If I did not know about God and Sin, would I go to Hell?" The priest answers: "No, not if you did not know." So the Eskimo says: "Then why did you tell me?"

It serves us to examine every single thing we have been told about God and ask ourselves: "Is it true?" Every belief you have about God is a storyline unless it can be verified by direct experience. Every thought that comes between you and God is a lie that prevents you from knowing the glorious truth.

Truth is neither doctrine nor dogma. Truth can only be known in the moment it is experienced. Jesus had direct experience of Truth ... but he was not a Christian. Mohammed had direct experience of Truth ... but he was not a Muslim. And so did Buddha ... but he was not a Buddhist. Every religion contains the seed of Truth. But a system of beliefs and laws grew up around Truth in a vain attempt to keep the flame alive as it got passed down from generation to generation. It's like Chinese Whispers in which a phrase is passed around from person to person. By the time its gets to the last person it has been distorted beyond recognition.

Truth can only be an honest encounter with *this* moment. In the experience of Truth all beliefs collapse and all that remains is the crystal-clear seeing of open awareness. In Truth you will see that God has no religion. God has no beliefs about how you should behave, what you should think, say or do. God does not have a code of conduct He lives by nor does He want you to have one. In Truth you will see that God is neither a person nor a thing and therefore He does not exist outside of you.

God is not something you can search for. God is what happens when you drop the search, when all separation between inner and outer dissolves to reveal Life *as it is now*. When you no longer need to ask who or what God is, His true identity is revealed to you. God is a moment-to-moment experience.

God is *what is*. God is Life itself.

Celebration of Life

When you drop the storylines about who or what you think God is, your life transforms beyond belief. Living the truth of clear-seeing transmutes the Fear of God to the Love of Life. And when you truly love Life, you have no choice but to celebrate.

Living in celebration means there's a deep devotion to *this* moment: every experience – mundane or sublime – is sacred. Wherever you are – standing at the kitchen sink or sitting at the feet of a saint – is the temple through which you enter to find God. And Life – as it is lived through you – becomes a prayer that has the capacity to take you right into the heart of Being. When you truly love Life, you become religious.

True religiousness is not a static teaching but a living mystery, a celebration of *what is*. I used to think that being religious meant being a devout Christian. At one stage in my life I had a strong desire to live a contemplative life as a nun but I was afraid that I'd have to give up an inquiring mind and believe a load of superstitious mumbo jumbo. Later on I was drawn to Buddhism but was repelled by the idea of adhering to a strict religious code that was unverifiable by my own direct experience. Disillusioned by the idea of religion – or any belief system that claimed to have the key to Heaven – I finally stopped believing even in God and devoted myself to the search for what is true.

After a while I noticed that Life had an uncanny habit of showing me where I still held onto fear-based ego. Whether it was my self-protective responses to the man in my life or my anxiety around dealing with financial issues, I noticed that the slightest retraction from the naked truth of what is created a sense of isolation that became unbearable as time went on. One day I decided that I had wasted enough time hiding in the shadows of my own smallness and made a vow that I would drag myself kicking and screaming into the glaring spotlight of *this* moment even though the weight of my habitual resistance pulled me in the opposite direction. I realized that I did not need to pray for redemption at a church altar nor did I need to surrender to a spiritual master: all that was required was that I sacrifice my ego on the altar of *this* moment and each moment. Life became my only guru and I became a devoted disciple. It marked a turning point in my life.

In deep union with Life itself, there's a Holy Marriage that gives birth to the Christ within, to our inner divinity. It's the same as our Buddha-nature and it's the same as our Godliness. God is an internal experience of at-onement, a return to our innate wholeness. So many wars have been fought to defend God's One and Only Religion. And each religion claims to be the Only One! They've been called Holy Wars, but how can war ever be holy? When we stop fighting with Life, all worldly battles will cease. When we stop fighting with ourselves, with others or with the world, we will experience our essential holiness.

And peace will reign on Earth once more. Now isn't that cause for celebration?

Bursting the Bubble of Bliss

These days the search for enlightenment is popular. There's a wave of enthusiasm ushering in the birth of a Golden Era and increasing numbers of people from all walks of life are being swept up by it. Some are drawn to join a satsang circle with a modern-day master. Others prefer to explore more esoteric philosophies that draw on the wisdom channeled from higher planes of consciousness. And others gravitate towards one of the many new-age disciplines that have grown from a Goddess-centered spirituality. There's so much to choose from and so much potential for transformation. But whatever our preference, it's the promise of freedom from suffering that beckons us so compellingly.

It's not surprising that a vision of hope is emerging in today's times of extreme change and uncertainty. As you can see by this book, I too am one of those riding the crest of the wave. I too believe that the brightest day is preceded by the darkest hour. I too believe there's a dawning of a new world. But, if we're not careful, belief in a New Age that can save us from our current predicament can too easily replace the traditional belief in religious salvation.

The idea that enlightenment is an unending spiritual high in which nothing bad or painful happens is a pernicious one because it is so seductive. Who doesn't want freedom from pain? Who doesn't want endless bliss, joy and peace?

*The expectation that God / Spirit / Enlightenment will give us perfect health, wealth or happiness is a fantasy that prevents us from knowing the truth of **this** moment. For true freedom, the bubble of bliss has to be burst!*

It's the ultimate reward for having worked so hard at your spiritual practice! It's the prize for having awakened!

The attachment to freedom from pain is a classic pitfall on the spiritual path. Knowing this hasn't prevented me from falling for it though! There have been times when I have experienced moments of such devastating clarity in which the whole world has sparkled with divine potential and I have been awakened from the trance of ego-induced horizontality. And there have been times when I have experienced Life as a magnificent river of grace in which I am one with everything and I have believed myself to be enlightened. And then I'd come up against another dark edge of fear and I'd think I was utterly deluded because I still carry my wounds and my life is still far from perfect. Even when I was sure I had dropped the whole idea of enlightened perfection, somewhere in the recesses of my mind I held onto a thread of hope that by just dropping the search all my problems would vanish.

The expectation that God / Spirit / Enlightenment will give us perfect health, wealth or happiness is a fantasy that prevents us from knowing the truth of *this* moment. For true freedom, the bubble of bliss has to be burst! I no longer know whether I am awakened or enlightened. And I no longer care. What I do know is that as soon as I think there is a destination I invariably fall off my high horse. And what I do care about is how best I can serve Life by staying deeply present in *this* moment.

You've got to be prepared for nothing to change. You've got to let go of all expectations, all dreams of unending bliss. I still get impatient when I feel like I have too much to do and time seems to be running out. I still get hurt when someone I open up to misunderstands me. And, at times, I can be defensive, contrary and clumsy in how I express myself. These are traits that have followed me since childhood.

Maybe one day they will just vanish like a balloon that has been popped. And maybe not. I seem to care less and less because I know myself to be much vaster than these surface details of my personality. And because there is a different quality to life these days.

I'm no longer a victim of circumstances. I no longer feel I'm being punished because I am a bad person nor do I blame Life for what hardships I may come against. Life simply is the way it is and by choosing to stay open amidst the horror and the beauty of it, I get closer to the truth of my divine essence. Occasionally I might argue with how things are, but very quickly I realize the futility of this and allow God's will to be done. The more honestly present I can stay in *this* moment and the more softly open I can be in *every* moment, the more my life gets illuminated by the radiance of God's love.

These days I figure what might be called enlightenment is an on-going deepening into *now*. It's like free-falling out of a plane except you never hit the ground. Far from being scary, it's wonderfully liberating. Once you learn to surf the current it gives you wings to fly!

So many times I've heard someone say: "Oh I can't be spiritual now, I can only access Spirit when I'm in Nature,

when I'm in stillness, when I'm dancing, when I've found the
right teacher, when I ..." I say: "What are you waiting for?"
Waiting creates another barrier between you and the truth
of your radiant nature. Waiting to be somewhere other than
where you are prevents you from seeing that everything is
spiritual exactly *as it is*. There is no place but *here* and there
is no time but *now*.

Let yourself fly so that you may be set free.

Beyond Death

Getting right up close and intimate with Life brings us into
right relationship with God. It heals the fracture at the core
of all suffering and brings us into right relationship with
every aspect of our lives.

When we embrace the fullness and depth of *this* moment
as it is *now*, the struggle for survival is negated. Even
though life has its ups and downs, its unexpected challenges
and hardships, we no longer fight against it. In allowing
ourselves to meet *what is* in naked openness, life becomes
a divine dance in which we are willing to be obliterated

into God in every moment. The obliteration of all storylines pierces the veil of mystery that keeps God hidden from us in one fell swoop. Every moment offers us this opportunity to experience complete at-onement. And this includes the moment of death.

Death is not separate from Life even though every fiber of our being tells us it is. That's how ingrained our belief in death is. Everything we have been taught tells us that death is the end of Life. We are told that whilst our souls go to Heaven or Hell according to the verdict on Judgment Day, life as we know it is over. For most people who have not realized their essential nature this means that everything stops. Basically, consciousness is snuffed out. Just One Big Black Nothingness. Or is it?

Death might well be the opposite of birth but both are a part of Life: they are at either end of the same continuum.

The belief that death is the end of Life keeps the truth of our eternal nature hidden from us. It's probably the biggest lie we have fallen for.

The belief that death is the end of Life keeps the truth of our eternal nature hidden from us. It's probably the biggest lie we have fallen for. And one that has caused so much fear ... of both death and Life. It's the biggest obstacle that stands between us and God.

There's a way through though. Being brave enough to embrace Life in all its terror and all its delight brings with it an unexpected gift: we rediscover our immortal nature. The more intimate we get with Life, the more our fear of death evaporates. The more openly we stand in the translucence of *this* moment, the more we realize that what we truly are does not die but remains constant as the consciousness that experiences the *now*-ness of Life.

Life never ends. Whether you inhabit a physical vehicle or not is irrelevant. You know this when you enter deeply through the gateway of the body, when you experience the formlessness within form. When you are fully present in *now*, you experience time as an endless series of moments. This is the same as in Life. Just as there is no beginning or end to time, there is no beginning or end to Life. Just as the river of Love continues to flow when a relationship ends, so does Life continue when our earthly existence is over.

It's only our small self that thinks love has died or Life has ended. Time is eternal. Love is eternal. Life is eternal. Birth and death are neither the beginning nor the end of Life but portals through which we pass in order to experience the glory of our eternal nature.

In every moment you are given the opportunity to die into God. You can choose to close in fear – and harden into the contours of who you *think* you are – or you can open as love – and expand into the vast awareness that you *really* are. In choosing love, the lie of small self dies and you are reborn as the truth of your infinite essential self. The power to make this choice is yours even at the moment of death.

You can open to the miracle of death as you can open to the miracle of Life. Just as you co-create your reality on the material plane, you are the author of your experience on the spiritual plane. Your inner world – in other words, your core beliefs about life and death – is what remains constant and you carry this with you when you pass through the portal of death. It's just a matter of changing perspective. You can choose to hold tight to the limitations of ego. Or you can let go and let God.

In deep surrender to death – as in deep surrrender to

silent awareness – you disappear and God is revealed. And God is who you are.

Heaven on Earth

There is no Heaven or Hell in the After-Life, only Heaven and Hell on Earth. Death – and life – is of our own making and the evidence points to the fact that we have mostly chosen to create a hellish world. Just look at how we maim, kill and torture innocent people in the name of political and religious justice. Just look at how we inflict unimaginable suffering on defenseless animals in the name of scientific progress. Just look at all the famine, poverty and disease two-thirds of the world's population endures on a daily basis.

But it is not God who is responsible for Good and Evil on Earth ... it is us! Only we have the power to change our world. There's no point waiting for God to sort it out because He is whatever is. Whilst the transformation happens on the inner plane by taking the leap from our heads to our hearts, nothing will change on the outer plane unless we put that transformation into good use through our physical actions.

God gave us bodies so that we can carry out His will. And His will is whatever we will it to be. If we choose war, violence and crime ... so be it. And if we choose peace, kindness and respect ... so be it. Our suffering is of our own making. And so is our salvation.

The realization of our own divinity grants us the power to make new choices. Once we know who we really are, we cannot fail to choose Love. How could God choose separation if He is Unity itself? Likewise, how could we choose fear if we know we are God?

When we realize that we – like God – are eternal, we will naturally grow out of the immaturity of self-centeredness. The accumulation of money, possessions and power without regard for the effect on others, the world or the planet is a short-term view that keeps us locked into an infantile relationship with Life. It is a co-dependent attitude that puts a stranglehold on the miracle of Love. Knowing we are God

God gave us bodies so that we can carry out His will. And His will is whatever we will it to be.

moves us into a higher perspective in which we can see that our actions, words and thoughts have a long-range effect on everything that exists. It's like the "butterfly effect" in chaos theory in which a single flap of a butterfly's wing in Brazil sets off a tornado in Texas.

It is not only our children and our grandchildren who will suffer if we make myopic choices today. We also will suffer. Our souls keep returning to the earthly domain to experience the joy of remembering we are co-creators of our reality. What sort of world will we come back to if we keep on being selfish? Our legacy to future generations is our legacy to ourselves. We are the ones who inherit the future ... for better or for worse.

When each of us understands that *God is all there is* and *we are God*, the lie of separation that our world is built on will dissolve. All material, political, economic and social structures that uphold a horizontal view of reality will crumble and in their place will be born a new world built on Love and Truth. This is the new vertical paradigm emerging from the depths of today's troubled times.

You – and I – have the power to create Heaven on Earth. We cannot afford to wait for one moment longer. Let us remember our own radiance so that we can bring light where there is darkness. We are – each and every one of us – spiritual beings of infinite magnitude. We always have been and always will be. Let us not forget ever again.

Entering the Gateway of Spirit

I invite you to close your eyes now and take one small step into the temple of your consciousness. Nowhere to go, nothing to search for … just being here.

Allow yourself to bask in the pristine perfection of *this* eternal moment. Absolutely naked, innocently open. Allow yourself to let go completely, falling into the very heart of Being. Let yourself die into *this* moment, let everything that you *think* you are simply fall away. Hold onto nothing! No form, no thought, no space, no time. Let yourself go into the vastness that is beyond all that is known to you.

Give up everything that is not *this*! Sacrifice everything for *now*!

It may feel scary initially because you think that everything that you are will come to a terrible end. You fear the death of your identity. But in allowing yourself to dissolve into the emptiness of not knowing who you are, you will discover that what lies beyond form is far more fantastic than anything you could ever imagine. Let yourself die moment by moment. Free fall into the void of formlessness. Nothing to hold onto ... just being here *now*!

Give up everything that is not *this*! Sacrifice everything for *now*!

Just this one small step inside is all it takes to be reborn as the One Consciousness That Is All. Just this one small step inside would be a giant step if each of us took it. It heralds the next stage in the evolution of humanity in which we will know ourselves as God.

Let's take this step together ... *NOW!*

Afterword
Where do we go from here?

When I started writing this book I had no idea I would be talking about something as radical as God. What began as an invitation to step onto the path of spiritual awakening has ended up as a call to inquire into the nature of the most challenging, contentious, misaligned and misunderstood concept in the whole world.

I was sent a letter not long ago by someone who demanded I take God out of the title of my book because it would put off too many readers. And I frequently come up against a stony wall of silence when I tell people what I am writing about.

But whenever I have shied away from using the God word I have received clear nudges from Existence to stop pussyfooting around and brave the storm. When I finally accepted that God was here to stay, everything fell into place.

As the words tumbled onto the page, I found myself repeating the same message given to us by such luminaries at the forefront of the new spirituality as Neale Donald Walsch, Marianne Williamson, Eckhart Tolle, Byron Katie and others. These spiritual teachers tell us – each in their own inimitable way – that we have the power to liberate ourselves from suffering by knowing the truth that is within us. Whilst each has a different name for this – God, Love, Being, Presence, Translucence, What Is – they are referring to the same thing. We need to hear this message in as many ways as possible and each time it is presented anew there is a freshness and immediacy that cannot fail to touch perhaps a few more people around the world. God knows this needs to happen!

Of course, there's nothing really new here: it's an age-old wisdom at the core of all spiritual traditions. But what is truly radical is that today this truth is accessible to everyone. It is not – as it has been in the past – the privilege of a few rare individuals. Why is this? Well, on the one hand, this wisdom is no longer cloaked in mysterious language. On the other hand, maybe we are developing the ears to hear it. And what is truly extraordinary is that, although numbers are still relatively few, more and more ordinary people are "getting it". More and more people are waking up from the spell of ego and living life from an expanded perspective with more presence, more joy, more compassion and a renewed purpose.

Even though many people's eyes still glaze over at the mere mention of the word God, I get the sense that there are also many more people who are willing to examine their beliefs about what God means. I get the sense that consensus reality is beginning to show cracks through which we can get a glimpse of the bigger picture, and that an increasing number of people are more ready than ever to make a connection to the divine. I recently saw a billboard over a US highway that tickled me. On a huge plain black background was printed in simple white lettering: "We need to talk. – God." Certainly it's a dialogue that is long overdue!

I have a strong feeling that human consciousness is about to make an evolutionary leap. And it could be as radical

More and more people are waking up from the spell of ego and living life from an expanded perspective with more presence, more joy, more compassion and a renewed purpose.

as the emergence of life from inanimate matter billions of years ago. All the signs are here. Scientific evidence shows that unprecedented technological advances have occurred in an incredibly short space of time. Statistical evidence shows that humanity has reached a point of "maximum exponential growth". Sociological evidence shows a shift from looking for material solutions to economic, political and environmental problems to looking for answers from within. And world myths originating in many cultures – such as Hindu, Buddhist, Chinese, Mexican and Mayan – describe a new world age that is about to come.

All this points to the likelihood of a dramatic change in humanity's existence. Barbara Marx Hubbard, the visionary and futurist, has called it the birth of *Homo Universalis*, the

Universal Human who is "connected through the heart to the whole of life." Osho called it the dawn of *Homo Novus*, the New Man who is "both earthy and divine, both worldly and otherworldly." We stand on an exciting threshold!

So where do we go from here? Well, let us each remember that we are all connected and that times are such that God speaks through each and every one of us. Let us remember that we are each His Divine Messengers and that the expression of divinity occurs in both big and small ways. Whatever it is that we are doing, we can serve Life by embracing the fullness and depth of *this* moment *as it is now*. Wherever we are, we can be courageous enough to reveal the truth of an open heart and inspired enough to put love into action. Let us remember as we go about our daily business that every interaction we have is a holy one.

And let us remember that we do not need to look for God. God is *right here*, writing this book ... and reading it! Whoever we are, we can be agents of change.

Will you join me in being a part of the revolution of consciousness that is happening *now*?

To find out more, go to www.AmodaMaaJeevan.com.

SEVEN GATEWAYS TO GOD
Guided Meditations from
How to Find God in Everything

Amoda Maa Jeevan takes you on a beautiful journey to your own divine essence with these seven guided meditations woven into an ambient soundscape specially created by her partner Kavi.

Available on www.AmodaMaaJeevan.com